THE INVISIBLE HAND

BOOKS BY THE SAME AUTHOR:

Go Watch TV
What and How Much Should Children Watch?

He Loved and Served

Spirit in Action

To a Seeker

Corinne True

To Be One: A Battle Against Racism

Winning Spiritual Battles

Education on Trial

ACKNOWLEDGMENTS

While I had to write this book, I also knew I needed help doing it. Maintaining sharp focus of this book's theme was a challenge. After all, I am far from being a seer.

The writings of Shoghi Effendi were extremely helpful in providing me with an understanding of where humanity is heading, and how it will get there. The oral and written commentaries of Jane Faily, Hussein Danesh, Peter Khan and Thelma Khelghati were helpful as well.

I am also grateful to Michael Morgan and Carroll Robbins for their efforts in editing the manuscript, and Chester Makoski, Jr., for designing the book's cover.

Images International's generosity in allowing me to review many of its audiotapes that deal with the theme of this book is deeply appreciated.

Special thanks, too, to Craig Harmsen who coordinated the technical production of the book. And without my wife's (Carol) continued encouragement to write it, it would never have been done.

Nathan Rutstein
Amherst, Massachusetts
April, 1992

The Invisible Hand

Shaping The New World Order

by

Nathan Rutstein

WHITCOMB
PUBLISHING

TABLE OF CONTENTS

Introduction

As a journalist during the height of the Cold War, I remember the term "Domino Effect" being used by world affairs analysts. It was used especially in reference to the Vietnam War. Should South Vietnam fall to the North Vietnamese, they felt, every other Southeast Asian nation would fall as well.

Well, South Vietnam did fall to the Communists, but most of the other nations in Southeast Asia didn't follow suit.

As for the Domino Effect theory? It didn't die with the end of the Vietnam War. In time, a stunned humanity witnessed the Domino Effect in the most unlikely place - Eastern Europe. And it wasn't triggered by military aggression.

Prior to the dismantling of the Berlin Wall, the world's two superpowers decided to end their arms race. It was as if some mighty invisible hand had applied the emergency brake to mankind's mad dash to self-annihilation Several major disarmament treaties followed. Then one nation after another - in rapid succession - broke away from the Soviet block . And not long after Poland, Hungary, Czechoslovakia, Rumania and Bulgaria freed themselves of the Kremlin's iron grip, the Soviet Union began to disintegrate. First the Baltic States broke away. In a matter of months, Soviet communism died; and weeks later the USSR no longer existed.

During the whirlwind period of unprecedented change in world affairs, the Cold War was officially declared over. Because most of us were brought up during the Cold War era, it was difficult to believe that it no longer existed. We were like the person who loses an arm and continues to sense its existence.

Caught by surprise, the great geopolitical analysts and news commentators tried to explain what led to the dramatic changes in the world. But their retrospective explanations were woefully feeble. And the honest ones admitted it.

With the dissolution of the Cold War, there was serious talk of a new world order emerging. While some observers gained glimpses of what that would be like, most people remained mystified by the concept. In fact, it scared lots of them, who, over the years, had adjusted to the familiar old world order patterns, trying to make the best of it. They feared the unknown.

On the other hand, there were a few men and women who had picked their way out of the wreckage of the Cold War, and noticed that humanity was on an irrevocable course toward world unity; that the nation-state was no longer a viable geopolitical entity. Some modern-day visionaries have written about the social, economic and political metamorphosis taking place in the world. The Club of Rome, a distinguished futurist think tank, addresses this planetary transformation in its report, *The First Global Revolution:*

"We are convinced that we are in the early stages of the formation of a type of world society, which will be different from today's as was that of the world ushered in by the Industrial Revolution from the society of the long agrarian period that preceded it."

What has happened in recent times didn't surprise the Baha'is. The term "new world order" is a familiar one. They anticipated the coming together of the Eastern and Western hemispheres, and the inevitable internationalization of our planet, a divine process that would lead to the establishment of world peace. This is all part of the vision of the founder of their Faith - Baha'u'llah.

As a Baha'i I am aware of the vision. But I'm also aware of the present-day uncertainty expressed by most people in relation to the unexpected changes that have taken place, and are still taking place in the world. Even many of the so-called world affairs experts remain perplexed. I remember as a journalist how their opinions regarding the durability of the Cold War conflicted with my religious beliefs. There were moments when I had doubts.

This book is an attempt to share with people, who are unfamiliar with the Baha'i vision, an explanation of what led to the world-shaking, unexplainable series of events that had been prophesied by Baha'u'llah in the mid-19th century.

My hope is that after examining the explanation, the reader will be less anxious about the future, will have a better understanding of where humanity is headed, and will have some idea of what the future global society - the new world order - will be like.

1
Cold War - A Real War

As long as I could remember, war was being waged somewhere in the world. In the mid-1930s Japan was raping China and the Spanish Civil War was raging. A few years later the Finns and Russians were engaged in battle; and then the big one, World War Two, which affected every continent and generated nightmarish memories that I and I'm sure, millions of others who lived through it will never forget. When finally the atomic bombs were dropped on Hiroshima and Nagasaki, the horrors of Auschwitz and Pearl Harbor were suddenly overshadowed by the sight of the towering mushroom clouds over Japan. The prospects of nuclear conflagration made us aware that humanity had the means of annihilating itself.

Haunted by that prospect, we tried to make the best of a precarious situation by trying to convince ourselves that our leaders were too sensible to engage in a nuclear conflict. For a moment we allowed ourselves the luxury of fantasizing about a world without war. But even after the United Nations was established, we grew more uncertain about our chances of avoiding a global holocaust. The evidence was overwhelming that World War Three was inevitable. Thinking about what another world war would be like was too horrible to contemplate. Yet, it was difficult not to think about it.

At almost every turn we were reminded that real peace - the kind we dreamed would materialize after World War Two - didn't exist. It wasn't the anti-colonialist struggles in Indochina, Algeria, the Congo and the Dutch East Indies that frightened us very much. Nor did the war between India and Pakistan, not the stubborn, ongoing Israeli-Arab conflict. None of those countries had "the bomb." Besides, those scrapes simply confirmed our suspicion that wherever humans lived there would be differences of opinion that would eventually explode into violent confrontations. While we attributed that belief to human nature, we still held out some hope that maybe one day "swords would be beaten into ploughshares."

What really scared us was kept locked deep down inside us. It was the illusion of peace our leaders tried to weave. And what compounded that fear was our reluctance to challenge our leaders' assumption that, because the world's superpowers weren't dropping atom bombs on each other, we were experiencing peace. We didn't know what to believe. Part of us wanted to accept the illusion as reality, because we yearned for peace in the worse way; but another part of us - the real us - knew all along that we were clinging to a phantom.

There was no peace of mind. At the height of the Korean War, shock waves of fear flashed throughout the world when some American senators and generals called for a nuclear strike in order to break the battlefield stalemate and vanquish the enemy. Fortunately, President Harry Truman, who had ordered the atomic attacks on Hiroshima and Nagasaki, rejected the plea. Yet, the Korean war had drawn humanity to the edge of disaster - fueling our paranoia, which was a private and painful phenomenon, something we refused to acknowledge in public.

Our paranoia intensified as we listened to Winston Churchill declare that an "Iron Curtain" separated the world into two sides - East and West. In the East, an emerging colossus - the Communist community of nations; in the West, the powerful and proud capitalist-oriented nations. Both sides assured of the righteousness of their cause, both sides determined to press forward their belief that they, and they alone, represented the best interests of humanity. The atmosphere was charged with threats and counterthreats, with hateful rhetoric.

At no time was the rhetoric stronger, and our fears more intensified, than when the Cuban missile crisis drew us once again to the brink of a nuclear war. When the Soviet Union set up missile stations in Cuba, the United States demanded that they be removed. The Kremlin countered: "Remove your missiles from Turkey, which borders the Soviet Union, and we'll do likewise in Cuba." Washington rejected the idea. As the two superpowers tested each other's nerve for several terrifying days, President John F. Kennedy decided to order an air strike, fully aware that it would most likely precipitate World War Three. Fortunately, the Soviets capitulated before the White House order was actually issued.

The images of the Cold War Era were just beginning. Television, having entered into the lives of almost every American, exposed us to the likes of Soviet Premier Nikita Khrushchev banging on a table and declaring that communism would eventually bury the West. We watched Soviet tanks crushing freedom uprisings in Hungary and Czechoslovakia, and we saw American troops torching Vietnamese villages and killing Vietnamese civilians.

The Vietnam War led East and West into what became commonly known as simply "the arms race." Both sides tested hydrogen bombs, weapons far more deadly than what obliterated Hiroshima. The production and refinement of nuclear weaponry escalated, producing inter-continental missiles that could be fired from land and submerged submarines. The sight of a missile knifing through the surface of the sea, shooting through the sky, heading for a pre-determined target was an image painfully preserved by us. Attempts to forget usually failed because our psyches had been etched with a fear that humankind might destroy itself. The erection of the Berlin Wall, with armed guards perched on enclosed towers, peering through binoculars, showed us that the Cold War was a real war.

As the Cold War intensified, desperate men created a new form of warfare - one which transcended national boundaries and ignored the established Geneva Convention rules of war. Terrorism scared us all. What bothered us more than reports of suicidal attacks on American installations in Lebanon was the everyday psychological trauma which terrorism generated everywhere. It intensified our paranoia. We didn't know when the next attack would take place. No spot seemed safe. Everyone became a potential target. Passenger planes were blown up in midair; others were hijacked and passengers taken hostage; luxury liners were seized and passengers killed; bombs were planted in mailed packages. All of that, and more, along with the omnipresent fear of a nuclear holocaust and the accelerated deterioration of the planet's ecological system, forced many of us to become hypersensitive regarding our community's security and our personal survival.

As East and West accused each other of global expansionism, they secretly conspired to overthrow regimes that were friendly to the other side. It turned out to be a bloody geopolitical chess game, with the CIA and the KGB adroitly moving the pieces. Some of their escapades burst into full scale wars - like in Vietnam and Afghanistan. All of this going on while the United States and her allies and the Soviet Union and her allies were amassing enough nuclear weapons to blow up our planet several hundred times. Though we were aware of that dreadful information, we were terribly frustrated, because we were helpless in putting an end to the accelerating arms race. We knew how vulnerable human beings are to making mistakes; someone with top security clearance in the East or West could push the wrong button and set off a hail of nuclear missiles that would trigger a similar response from the enemy. No voice of reason or compassion could stop our lemming-like rush to extinction.

Many of us had no alternative but to try to repress our fears by anesthetizing ourselves with heavy doses of television, alcohol, drugs, food and sex; we tried to turn life into a never ending carousel of fun. But seeking fun was no fun. Not if you read newspapers, watched TV or listened to the radio. Those of us who pondered in private what was happening in the world wept deeply. It seems the deeper we thought, the more we cried. The fears we tried to run away from stayed with us. Many who couldn't take the heartache succumbed to the lure of drugs and alcohol or retreated to the mountain top. A "live-for-today only" attitude prevailed - hedonism turned into an elixir. It wasn't only the stressful worldwide geopolitical condition that frightened us. It was the swift changes that were taking place that made the Cold War era not just a concept to describe relations between East and West, but an assault on the very nature of being human.

Throughout World War Two, Americans were taught to hate the Germans and the Japanese and to love the Soviet Union. Shortly after the war, Japan and the Federal Republic of Germany were among America's closest allies and the Soviet Union its number-one enemy. I had difficulty making the adjustment, for the black and white moving pictures of mounds of corpses found in German-operated concentration camps had been permanently pressed into my consciousness. I don't think I'll ever forget those pictures; nor the pictures of thousands and thousands of

German and Austrian men, women and children expressing a worship-like adoration of a beaming Adolph Hitler sieg-heiling in all directions. How could a people who produced a Beethoven and a Goethe embrace the ideology of such a dictator? I wondered. It was difficult to forgive. The fact that the majority of churchmen in Germany either endorsed Hitlerism or did nothing to oppose it fueled my bitterness and anger.

With a new era, we had new enemies. In America, we had to hate the Russians, who fought so valiantly and suffered so much during the big war. And in the Soviet Union, the Russians had to hate Americans, the very same people who risked their lives throughout World War Two supplying them with food, clothing and weapons. I'll never forget the pictures of Russian men, women and children displaying their gratitude for the aid. I remember feeling, as a 13-year-old, that I had brothers and sisters across the sea. Five years later that feeling had to be abandoned or submerged in order to avoid being branded a "Commie" - a term that was synonymous with heretic in America. Ironically, very little made sense in a period of great technological advancement. It seemed like overnight we had computers, transistor radios, communication satellites in the sky, cable TV, fiberoptics, CAT-Scan machines replacing exploratory surgery procedures; heart, kidney, liver and lung transplants; men walking on the moon and satellites exploring planets millions and millions of miles away. Never had so much been invented in such a short period of time. It was a remarkable display of what human brain power could achieve.

While it was wonderful thinking about the future, there were many of us who wondered if there would ever be a future. Sure we were dazzled by all of the inventions that were helping some of us live more comfortably; but what really mattered wasn't happening - no amount of human brilliance was able to remove our fear of planetary extinction. Mass murdering techniques were becoming more and more sophisticated. The best minds were being incited to build bigger and better bombs and more efficient defense mechanisms; military scientists and government officials proclaimed that the weapons they were creating were necessary to keep the peace. Many of us wanted desperately to believe them. But what our leaders weren't aware of was how damaging the Cold War was to most of us - in the East and West. It had nothing to do with losing a leg, an arm or eye or being shot dead. It had to do with being disoriented, with pretending that everything was okay when deep down we knew it wasn't;

it had to do with damaged psyches, with a deadening of the human spirit.

While most of us never made the connection between the Cold War and the psychological trauma many people were experiencing, there were lots of symptoms: the high rise in suicides, especially among young people; the growing demand for cocaine, crack and heroin and alcohol; the AIDS epidemic sweeping across the planet; the sense of hopelessness and depression that permeated every strata of society. The high cost of maintaining the most sophisticated military force possible was causing internal domestic problems in the East and West. There wasn't enough money to care properly for the aged and ailing, to improve the failing quality of education, to repair the growing number of deteriorating highways and bridges; to overcome poverty, and the mushrooming social problems that resulted from it.

As a child I knew what a 'bum" was. He was a drifter, usually an alcoholic who congregated with others like himself in a special place called Skid Row. But as the Cold War dragged on - and no end was in sight - the number of bums increased. They were no longer only old and grizzly men; there was a growing number of women and teenagers among them, including impoverished families who couldn't make it with only welfare help, or were too proud to take a handout. They fanned out through the community, scavenging trash and garbage cans in neighborhoods that had never seen bums before. They slept in bus and railroad terminals, in playgrounds, on park benches, on sidewalks bordering fancy shops and malls. They became so commonplace that children nonchalantly stepped over them without glancing down. Sociologists gave them a new name - the homeless. In America alone there are quite possibly one million of them.

Many of these souls were victims of the Cold War: men, women and children who couldn't take the pressure that growing anxiety and fear and greed and selfishness generates. They never made a war office's casualty list. They were never given a Purple Heart. They had no special place to heal their deep interior wounds. They were outcasts that many of us who were busily involved in "getting ahead" and staying alive considered, at best, a nuisance. There were other outcasts - like the chronically poor, who sociologists in the 1990s have classified as the "underclass." Those materially deprived souls, cut off from the mainstream of society, were part of a cycle of poverty and social neglect that extended so far back that it had become an accepted way of life. They scavenged the garbage dumps of Manila; they slept on the streets of Calcutta; they lived in rotting tenements in Harlem, and the shantytowns that ring Rio de Janeiro and Nairobi and hundreds of other cities in rich and poor lands.

Most of us who were considered fine upstanding citizens pretended we had no wounds, working feverishly not to think too deeply lest we acknowledge them. We were afraid to face them, because we knew they weren't the kind of wounds that could be healed with a pill. Deep down we felt there wasn't anything that could be done to heal them; that truth was too painful to ponder, so we avoided thinking about it; and even devised intricate ways of burying it in some submerged corner of our minds - and rushed to join, or create new escapist adventures. To keep our sanity, we were forced to forget the truth, and try to construct a more manageable "truth," one that would bring joy into our lives. While it brought us moments of pleasure, it never succeeded in making us joyful. We, too, were victims of the Cold War. But unlike the homeless and the underclass we masked our pain, a maneuver that, in the long run, would prove to be more damaging. At least it seemed that the homeless and the underclass lived the truth.

The Cold War was a real war. It was real because it inflicted damage - lots of it. Wars do that sort of thing. Except that the kind of damage the Cold War inflicted was different. It was far more psychological than physical. Healing its victims was a problem. For how do you overcome a sense of hopelessness that people try to ignore or refuse to recognize? Overcoming a delusion often requires greater effort than solving the problem itself. The hopelessness that resulted from the Cold War didn't only affect Americans and Russians; those living in lands that weren't officially involved in the East-West struggle were also affected. The poisonous mist of hopelessness permeated every human domain. We were in the throes of a worldwide catastrophe and didn't know it.

How did hopelessness affect us? We were consumed by fear and uncertainty and, for sanity's sake, refused to acknowledge it. That condition resulted in our excessive inward thinking, increased selfishness, indifference to others' suffering, greed, and an inordinate preoccupation with pleasure, because it made us feel - at the moment - secure. Acquiring material possessions became an obsession. Without concern, we resorted to cheating, lying, deceit , backbiting to get what we wanted. We behaved

7

like what professional cynics believed all along - that humans are basically selfish animals primarily desirous of satisfying their natural lusts. The Cold War did to us what no other war had ever done: It drew us away from our spiritual nature, forcing us to function as creatures beneath our prescribed station. We lost sight of our destiny.

2
Far-flung Battlegrounds

When I was a journalist - even while operating on an international level - I was too close to the Cold War to appreciate its disastrous psychological impact on humanity. The signs of hopelessness were everywhere, but I never linked them with the Cold War; nor did my colleagues. We dutifully covered and reported the mounting misery and madness in the world. I tried hard to keep from becoming cynical and consumed by pessimism. It was a difficult struggle, for we were exposed every work day to man's inhumanity to man, carried out in a variety of ways. We were paid to follow the action, to try to unearth the reasons for the action and report it as clearly and accurately as possible. Unlike the rest of the citizenry, we couldn't block out the happenings in the world.

Had we taken to heart all of what we observed we would have caved in emotionally. But there were cracks in our armor. You just can't completely dismiss the human suffering that you're exposed to day after day. I could understand why so many of my colleagues washed away their worries with whiskey, or were quick to snicker when confronted with idealistic philosophies which could bring peace to the world.

There were times when my own optimism wavered. As a Baha'i I was aware of my faith's teaching that by the end of this century the nations of the world would come together economically and politically and establish the means to end war. I didn't dare share this view with all of my fellow journalists for fear of being mocked. Those few colleagues with whom I shared my belief politely dismissed it as wishful thinking. I could understand their reactions. The empirical evidence didn't support the idea of world peace by the year 2000.

I had doubts, too, especially in 1968. It was a year I'll never forget. I'm sure others who worked in the news media then would always remember what happened that year. An avalanche of disastrous events rocked our world, and every one of them was a lead story. When three or four of them broke the same day, pandemonium broke out in the newsroom; regular working hours and eating procedures were abandoned. We often worked around the clock, driven by adrenaline, but during quiet moments we girded ourselves for another outburst of major news, wondering if we would ever again enjoy a long stretch of tranquillity. The calm never came. Though we thought we knew a lot about global affairs, we were mystified as to why there was this continuous tumult in the world.

There were a few moments of relief. The first came during an Apollo mission that year - I saw all of our planet in space. As I gazed at it in awe, all doubts that it was round evaporated instantaneously. It seemed like such a peaceful place. There were no signs of war, famine, racism and fear, conditions that I knew existed there, on this precious jewel in space. A feeling of hope enveloped me, superseding my knowledge of the troubles besetting our planet. I had blocked out all negative thoughts. While marveling at that incredible sight, I was struck by an insight that in an instant blossomed into a belief: Earth is really my country. But as the resplendent vision disappeared, when the spacecraft's camera was shut off, I sensed hope being drawn from me. I was being pulled back to the familiar.

Against a backdrop of prolific nuclear weapons testing, the Vietnam War intensified in ferocity. The Tet offensive wracked Vietnam with blood, grief and horror. The savagery of that conflict was symbolized by a scene we reported, in color and natural sound, on dinner-time television: A South Vietnamese police chief placed a revolver to the head of a Viet Cong suspect and pulled the trigger. The youth fell to the ground, his head streaked with blood and brain matter. At first we were too pleased to have secured such spectacular footage to appreciate the statement that scene had made. We had it, and our competition didn't.

In Europe, Soviet armor rolled into Czechoslovakia and crushed a freedom uprising, making the Iron Curtain an impregnable barrier. Chances

10

of an East-West accord seemed impossible, and the probability of a nuclear war loomed greater. There were coups d'état in the Congo, Peru, Iraq, Mali and Panama. A bloody civil war was raging in Nigeria. Greeks and Turks were still fighting on Cyprus. A rash of PLO attacks on Israeli airliners triggered a series of Israeli retaliatory assaults in Lebanon. The Soviet Union expanded its naval presence in the Mediterranean and replenished 90 percent of Egypt's weapons arsenal that was lost in the war with Israel a year before. Growing hostility between the Soviet Union and China forced both sides to increase their military forces along the long border they shared. The threat of a Chinese invasion of Taiwan still existed. In Guatemala, the U.S. ambassador was dragged out of his limousine and blasted with pistol and machine gun fire. In Kenya, Tom Mboya, that country's political bright light, was assassinated.

In America, two assassinations, occurring only two months apart, plunged the nation into a state of shock. Dr. Martin Luther King was murdered in Memphis, and U.S. Senator Robert Kennedy was gunned down in Los Angeles. The world's wealthiest and most powerful nation grieved. People everywhere were asking openly: "What is our world coming to?"

After Dr. King's assassination, there were riots in Washington, D.C., New York, Chicago, Detroit, Los Angeles, and 121 other cities. Enraged black men and women, fed up with their lot, sought vengeance for a system that had murdered their Moses. The majority of Americans watched - in horror. They were accustomed to seeing troops and police battle unstable masses in less developed countries, but not in their country, the "land of the free and the home of the brave." At first, they had difficulty believing what they were seeing, but when the rioting spread from city to city and only a few miles from the Capitol Building and the White House - they believed. There was a rush on gun stores. Vigilante groups were organized. The Ku Klux Klan was revived, gaining recruits outside of the South - its traditional base of operations. A Polish government-sponsored anti-Semitism campaign forced thousands of Jewish citizens to find permanent refuge in other lands. Reminiscent of the Nazi era, most people and institutions outside of Poland did little to intervene on behalf of the Jews.

In China, the regime's "Cultural Revolution" was in full swing. Literally millions of men, women and children suspected of bourgeois

11

thinking were taken from their homes and herded into camps in remote areas to undergo long ideological transformation programs. Many of those that resisted were executed, while the rest bowed to the will of their supreme leader, Mao Tse Tung, who seemed to cast a hypnotic spell over them. A chill swept over people in other lands when they saw on television masses of Chinese, all dressed alike, waving little red books and chanting in unison the praises of Mao.

Other dramatic events ensued. France exploded its first hydrogen bomb, becoming the world's fifth thermonuclear power. China exploded its second thermonuclear device. The earth around Pahute, Nevada, shook when the United States set off a one megaton underground thermonuclear blast that was 100 times more powerful than what exploded over Hiroshima. When North Korea seized the U.S. electronic spy ship Pueblo, the world became aware of the superpowers' sophisticated spying systems. Not only were the Americans and Soviets operating fleets of spy ships around the planet, they had spy satellites in space photographing in sharp detail enemy installations, including missile sites. If our enemy can check out our military capability from space, we thought, then they can check out everything else. We felt even more hemmed in than before, more restricted . The little freedom we enjoyed was threatened.

The reaction to the mounting pressure of one bleak event occurring after another turned into a horrific series of ongoing events that kept gaining momentum until merging into a full-blown social problem that political, educational and religious leaders were incapable of solving. The protest movement was born, composed mostly of youth. They cried for peace and justice, they wanted more than reform, they wanted complete change. Because there was no unanimity as to what should replace the established order, which was blamed for the tension and despair and danger in the world, the protesters took to the streets, giving the impression to many of being a bunch of wild-eyed anarchists.

University campuses became the spawning ground and target of the protests. Students at Columbia University seized five buildings, held several officials hostage for 24 hours and looted and wrecked the president's offices. Scores of similar protests followed across North America. In Mexico City, troops killed about 30 students in order to quell rioting. In Paris, students battled police for days, setting up barricades, flying red flags and hurling bombs and cobblestones that they had plucked out of the city's ancient roads. Similar rioting broke out in other European cities. In America, defiance against the government grew. The burning of the American flag by Americans became a familiar scene on television; so was the burning of draft cards. Such scenes infuriated most of the other Americans who were trying to make sense out of a chaotic world. It wasn't easy to do that, for they were aware of the East-West conflict and what danger that posed to their personal security. Many of them felt that the protests were weakening the West's position in its efforts to stem the tide of communism. In some respects their fear was justified because the KGB tried to exploit the social unrest in the United States in order to expedite what the Kremlin felt was the inevitable downfall of capitalism.

But the protests would have occurred without the help of Soviet agents. For young people - many of them from white middle class homes - were fed up living with the fear of imminent nuclear war. As long as they could remember, they had been haunted by that fear, which kept them in a perpetual state of despair. More time was spent attending radical political rallies than attending class. Unlike their parents, the youth and young adults had lost faith in their government and in their family's religion. In fact, they were angry at "The Establishment" and wanted to punish its institutions for failing them, for placing the planet in jeopardy of extinction. New paths to peace had to be forged, they felt.

In their search for change, youths expressed their disdain for the existing order by purposely rejecting the traditional norms of behavior and dress. Men grew long hair; women trashed their brassieres. Together they frolicked and sang songs of a better day that was coming. But beneath the youths' laughter was the ever-present current of impending doom. Their laughter was really a form of hysteria. Some tried to find peace in communes; but the majority mobilized to pull down the existing order.

They had some victories - which gave rise to the kind of euphoria that results from gaining something that you don't really expect to get. When Eugene McCarthy, a former senator-turned-poet/philosopher, announced his candidacy for the presidency, many of them cut their hair, put on brassieres and worked feverishly for him. They viewed McCarthy as a savior. His strong showing in the Democratic Party's New Hampshire primary, as well as the continuous protests against the Vietnam War in Washington, forced President Lyndon Baines Johnson to announce that he would not seek re-election. It was more than a victory for the peace protesters; it demonstrated that they had power, that they could make a difference, that through McCarthy they had found the force that would bring about peace in the world. They redoubled their efforts on his behalf and continued their nationwide protest campaign against war. For some students, Johnson's decision not to run and McCarthy's victory drew humanity two steps closer to nirvana.

The students were crushed when McCarthy failed to win the nomination - their star of hope had faded. Many of them were convinced that trying to gain what they wanted was impossible to secure from the existing political system and social order. The militants among them expressed their anger and frustration by holding demonstrations outside the Democratic Party's convention in Chicago. While the convention delegates were engaged in the democratic process of selecting a presidential nominee, the police outside the hall charged into the 5,000 demonstrators, wielding clubs. When the demonstrators fought back, the police intensified their assaults, at times losing control, clubbing innocent bystanders to the ground as well as demonstrators. Scores of men and women were injured, including 30 journalists. What happened on that hot August night in Chicago left the world aghast.

The peace protesters were growing desperate. It seemed like their search for ways to establish peace was running into one dead end after another. Time and time again their expectations were not being fulfilled. What hurt the most were the defeats that followed their few victories. They were losing patience. Extremists among them trumpeted a call for violence to achieve their ends. A few splinter groups were formed that bombed defense research labs and military installations. Although the great majority remained peaceful, there were times when they couldn't restrain themselves.

I witnessed one of those breakdowns. I was field producing coverage of one of the biggest peace demonstrations in Washington's history. There must have been close to 500,000 people marching, many of the women and children holding or wearing flowers in their hair. I remember standing in front of the Justice Building, and the attorney general peering down at the demonstrators from his third floor office window. There was a barricade in front of the building, and behind it troopers armed with rifles. The crowd started shouting, "Justice! We want justice!" The more they shouted the angrier they sounded. When some of them rushed the barricade, the soldiers fired tear gas canisters into the crowd, setting off plumes of white smoke. As the marchers retreated the soldiers kept firing more and more canisters. I ran with the crowd, coughing, tears running down my cheeks. A woman, carrying her infant child, stopped and turned toward the Justice Building and cried out, "You bastards!"

3

Time for a Miracle

On May 4, 1970, National Guardsmen fired into a group of anti-war demonstrators at Kent State University in Ohio, killing four students. I don't think I'll ever forget the sight of a distraught young woman on her knees, inches from a blood-splattered, motionless body, pointing to the soldiers dressed for battle, and shrieking what everyone else in the stunned crowd was wondering, "Why did you do that?"

The official response from Washington never really satisfied most Americans. We were forced to adjust to another tragedy. The best way to do that, we had learned, was by forcing ourselves to forget about the incident. Some of us rationalized the Kent State incident by saying to ourselves, "It could have been a lot worse - like an H-Bomb attack." No doubt about it, human annihilation remained our number-one fear. Though there was no satisfactory answer as to why the soldiers fired into the peace marchers, events occurring after the shooting provided us with some clues. Student militancy waned. In fact, the Students for a Democratic Society broke up into small, squabbling, ideological factions and lost substantial support among students and professors. Hounded by the FBI, the Black Panthers went underground. Depression seemed to envelop campuses everywhere. Those who were caught smiling were suspected of smoking pot - and many really were.

Traditionally, troubled people would seek solace in religion. But in the '70s churchgoing declined considerably in the mainstream Christian

17

denominations. Enrollments in theological seminaries shrank. A similar condition existed in Judaism and Islam. Divinity school scholars probed for the reasons for the decline. In the United States, a former Roman Catholic priest, in his book "The Encounter," argued that Islam, Judaism and Christianity had, by their exclusivism, spent their energies on self-interest and lost their credibility. The book was widely accepted as an accurate picture of the impotency of historic religion. Some people outwardly or secretly embraced the "God is dead" theory. To support their case, they pointed to the world's condition. If there was a God, they reasoned, all of humanity wouldn't be gripped by fear, girding itself for the inevitable nuclear attack. If there was a God, there would be peace. Many who remained faithful in their belief in God lost faith in religious institutions. Increasing reports of church corruption and clergymen committing immoral acts, in addition to the incessant feuding and fighting between religions and sects, were among reason why many men and women wanted nothing to do with organized religion. In Northern Ireland, Roman Catholics and Protestants were killing each other. Even direct intervention by the pope failed to end the shooting and bombing. In India, Hindus and Muslims were continually at each other's throats. In Sri Lanka, Buddhists and Hindus were engaged in a bloody feud. In the Middle East, Israeli Jews and Arab Muslims and Christians were locked in an ongoing war in which thousands of lives had been lost, and new casualties were being reported practically every day. Muslim nations were warring with one another. Iraq and Iran, each claiming that God was on its side, paid dearly in their 10-year ferocious struggle: One million soldiers lost their lives. To many highly educated people, religion was viewed as an anachronism. Whether they accepted communism or not, they appreciated Karl Marx's observation that "religion ... is the opium of the people."

Interestingly, while communism was fundamentally atheistic, it took on the trappings of a religion, gaining legions of converts - especially intellectuals - in the developing nations of Africa, Asia and Latin America. They tried to adopt the Soviet Union's pattern to success, for they noticed how quickly poverty, hunger and illiteracy were eliminated in that country. Communism was providing grassroots people with the kind of security in this life that established religion had failed to give them. In fact, religion was made out to be a tool of the colonialists, an instrument used

18

by the politically entrenched to maintain the status quo.

Though I was partial to the West's cause, I was impressed with communism's appeal to the downtrodden and impoverished of the world. It seemed to be the only logical way for them to improve their lot in a relatively short period of time. Khrushchev's threat now seemed more like a prophecy in the process of being fulfilled. I was also impressed with the Soviet Union's ability to assume superpower status so soon after World War Two, a time when Russia's industrial capability was devastated, its farmland scorched and many of its leading cities gutted. Its remarkable recovery - and the launching of the first manned space vehicle - were foreign policy bonanzas for the Soviet Union. They fueled the developing nations' desire to follow the path forged by the Russians to achieving national stability and solidarity.

What Mao Tse Tung was able to achieve through communism was also impressive. He united what was a hopelessly fragmented country, eliminating hunger and establishing a successful means of healing the sick and educating the masses. In the eyes of many men and women in the developing nations - especially youth and young adults - what was happening in the Soviet Union and China was a modern-day miracle. The West was losing the battle for the minds and hearts of the so-called Third World people - who were flocking to Marxism with religious zeal. When technologically-backward North Vietnam bloodied and booted super-power America out of Indochina, I realized that communism was going to be around for a long time. It was deeply entrenched, with great grassroots appeal.

The Cold War, it seemed, would last through my lifetime, maybe longer. That realization was in conflict with my religious belief - that the nations of the world would be united around the year 2000. For me, it was a test of faith, for how in God's name will the world be united by 2000, I wondered to myself, never daring to share my doubts with my fellow Baha'is. Only a miracle, I thought, could bring about peace by the end of the century, for, based on the prevailing global geopolitical situation, there were no signs of hostility diminishing between the United States and the Soviet Union. World affairs analysts agreed that the West was too powerful for the East to conquer, and vice versa. Both sides were embroiled in a feverish arms race, and unwilling to compromise on their rigid ideological positions.

While a godless religion was spreading rapidly throughout the developing world, some people in the West, especially in the United States, were turning to God, but not through conventional channels. Though they no longer went to church or synagogue, and even gave up their affiliation with them, they sought spiritual sustenance from other religious sources, sources most conservative Americans felt were cults. Zen Buddhism and I Ching were popular. So were certain religious expressions of Yoga. Interest in astrology continued to boom. The Moonies' dream of world brotherhood had appeal to youth yearning for some organization that had at least a vision of how peace could materialize. Clergymen of the established religious sector manifested their concern by either adopting some of the philosophy and practices of the new-age religious movements - hoping that that would keep the parishioners in the fold; or by vehemently attacking them as satanical forces.

The '70s were a time when the quest for truth was motivated, by and large, by a burning desire for peace. Many felt that when truth was discovered peace would automatically follow. Unfortunately, most sincere seekers didn't find what they were really looking for; instead, they found themselves swimming against a stiff current of conflicting viewpoints. People were tired of searching, of pondering, of evaluating, and even dreaming of a better day. It didn't help that President Jimmy Carter was aware of his country's deflated will and surrender to indifference. His television address to the nation, in which he declared that a grand malaise had overcome America, didn't shake Americans out of their apathetic stupor. In fact, his assessment of the American psychological condition was viewed by many of his fellow citizens as unpatriotic. His sharing of the truth contributed to his political downfall. It didn't matter that Carter had played a historic role in making significant headway in trying to end the bitter Israeli-Arab conflict.

Through the Camp David Accords, Egypt - the Arab world's leading military power at the time - and Israel forged diplomatic relations. People of good will everywhere were moved by the television scene of Egypt's Anwar Sadat and Israel's Menachem Begin shaking hands - and President Carter looking on, beaming with pride. But it didn't take long to forget that marvelous memory. Carter alienated many American farmers and businessmen when he instituted an embargo on grain shipments to the Soviet Union - his response to their decision to become militarily involved in

Afghanistan's civil war. He angered many more Americans when he was unable to free the U.S. diplomats who were being held hostage by Iran's Revolutionary Guards. With many Americans still smarting over the Vietnam defeat, Ayatollah Khomeni made the United States appear feeble in the eyes of the world. On the one hand, many Americans craved the chance to demonstrate its nation's might; on the other hand, there was the fear that military involvement might lead to another Vietnam.

Carter was blamed for America's slippage in prestige. The worsening of an already unfavorable international trade situation, double-digit inflation and soaring interest rates on bank loans were added strains on the beleaguered president - a man who had entered the White House viewed by many voters as the potential savior who would restore the honor to the station of the presidency that had been badly besmirched by the Watergate scandal. People were looking for honesty in government, an end to patronage and the political "good old boy" network. In Carter, they had seen a man of the soil, an extremely spiritually-minded person, an intelligent man of sterling integrity. While his admired characteristics weren't questioned, Carter was thrashed in his bid for re-election.

The American electorate yearned for a savior. The conservatives were seeking someone who would restore America's dignity, America's number-one position in the world; they sought someone who would also strengthen the nation's moral fiber and make its citizens proud of their country. The liberals were looking for someone who could get the world to agree on total disarmament, someone who could negotiate an end to the Cold War and eliminate poverty. Those in the political center wanted some of what the other two camps wanted.

When most Americans entered the voting booth in the 1980 presidential election, they were looking to cast a ballot for someone who could deliver them from the hopelessness they refused to openly acknowledge. That wish was possessed by most people in all strata of society and political camps. For most people the future seemed bleak. When reviewing humanity's performance in the past and present, they concluded that the future could only be worse. For example, Harvard biologist George Wald - a 1967 Nobel laureate - felt humankind was running out of time: "I think human life is threatened as never before on this planet. Many perils are coming to a head at about the same time. I am one of those scientists who finds it hard to see how the human race is to bring itself much past the year 2000."

Afraid to contemplate the future, most people committed themselves to getting as much as they could from each day they lived. Some religionists believed that route could only lead to sinful hedonism. Their reaction led to an upsurge of fundamentalism in Christianity, Islam, Judaism and Hinduism. By stressing what they believed to be the basics of their religion, they felt they were becoming acquainted with a spiritual essence that would provide them with the clear perspective and focus needed to lead a meaningful and fruitful life. It was also felt that by clinging to religious basics, they would experience the enthusiasm and certitude displayed by the early followers of the founders of their faith - thus becoming better human beings.

Religious fundamentalism generated a separatism between believer, who was viewed as righteous and sanctified, and non-believer, who was made to feel unclean, defiled, an agent of the devil. In America, fundamentalists set up their own schools, purchased their goods from stores operated by fellow religionists, and they tried to infiltrate the political arena by producing and promoting candidates with fundamentalist religious views. The intolerance exhibited by fundamentalists created a spirit of ill will in communities and a fanaticism that often times inflamed latent prejudices. Mainstream churchgoers were frightened by fundamentalist attitudes and behavior. And those who had given up on religion were convinced that they had done the right thing when witnessing the actions of the religious zealots.

In the Middle East, fundamentalism was being hailed as the wave of the future. Disillusioned idealists who had experimented with socialism, and pragmatists who had found the ways of the West lacking, were looking to fundamentalism to establish a more equitable, more secure and happier way of life. In Iran, they looked to Ayatollah Khomeni to perform the miracle they yearned for. When he engineered the overthrow of the shah, many Muslims were convinced they had witnessed a miracle; for, in spearheading the successful revolution, Khomeni had single-handedly overcome the opposition of the United States, the world's wealthiest nation. Inspired by Khomeni's triumph, Islamic radicals in other lands plotted the overthrow of their secular rulers, such as Egypt's President Anwar Sadat, who was assassinated by religious extremists.

Khomeni instituted severe changes in Iran, plunging his countrymen into an austere 10th century way of life that degraded the status of women, abolished the playing of music, launched a massive campaign to eliminate all outspoken and imagined opponents. A 10-year reign of terror was waged against the Baha'is, the largest non Muslim religious minority in Iran. Their cemeteries were desecrated, their centers and financial savings seized, their children kicked out of school, and Baha'i physicians and lawyers stripped of their licenses. Thousands of Baha'i men and women were imprisoned and tortured and hundreds were executed. Other religious minorities were also persecuted. Political opponents were either jailed - or eliminated.

In Lebanon, religion seemed to have gone mad, due partly to Khomeni's influence. Not only were Christians and Muslims locked in combat, but Islam's Sunni and Shiite sects were killing each other; even Shiite factions were shooting at one another - and the Druze were in the fray, fighting to repulse any encroachments by other sects upon their territory. Muslim clerics' master-minding the taking and torturing of hostages infuriated decent people everywhere.

I was appalled at what was going on in the name of God. Religion was supposed to be the cause of unity. In fact, the word religion stems from the Latin word *religio*, which means to bind together. During the Cold War era organized religion was, for the most part, the cause of discord and enmity, and was failing as a unifying agency. It was apparent to most discerning persons that churches were losing their influence with their membership. The gap between religious belief as a creed and religious practice as a way of life was widening. In Christianity, for example, the principle of turning the other cheek wasn't, in the main, practiced by Christians. The average parishioner preferred the "eye for an eye " principle. Not striking back was considered foolish.

4

Doom and Gloom

The weakening moral fiber and growing greed and fear in the world allowed individuals and institutions to seriously abuse our planet - polluting our air, our waterways, even the food we were growing. A grocery list of environmental concerns, from rain forest depletion to acid rain, frightened us. Every week, it seemed, there was some new discovery that caused us to worry about our planet. The industrial wastes (7 billion tons of toxins a year in the early '80s) generated in the United States and the ongoing disregard for conservation eliminated thousands and thousands of plant and animal species that had contributed to the maintenance of the Earth's balance of nature. Continued plant species extinction could lead to a depletion of oxygen in the atmosphere and endanger the production of life-saving medicines.

Nuclear power plant accidents in the United States and the Soviet Union - and the danger of that occurring again and again - worried us. So did the need to find places to safely discard nuclear waste, which takes thousands of years to deactivate.

The Earth's pollution problem was, in large measure, a byproduct of the Cold War. Staying ahead of the enemy in weapons production and economic strength was more important than having to put up with a little filth in the environment. Most people went along with their leaders' arguments, because their greatest concern was that their side be properly prepared to repel an enemy attack - and to avoid the unthinkable - losing

World War Three. Yet, they didn't dismiss the pollution problem altogether; it was simply relegated to their long list of lesser concerns.

The fact that the United Nations' influence in the world was waning didn't help matters. The enthusiasm for the organization that existed when it was first formed in 1945 was gone. At that time, the war-weary everywhere felt that the United Nations was going to turn swords into ploughshares, prevent countries from warring, and lead humanity to everlasting peace. Instead, it became a major diplomatic battlefield of the Cold War. The superpowers used the United Nations as a propaganda vehicle to denounce their enemies and a breeding ground for developing political allies. The fact that the United Nations was doing good work in combating disease and providing technical assistance to developing countries, went, for the most part, unnoticed in the developed communities. The low opinion of the United Nations in the industrialized West, in particular, was based on the fact that wars were raging on three continents and the United Nations was incapable of ending them. In the United States, many people viewed the world organization as a glorified debating society, where weaker nations had an opportunity to stand up to stronger nations, or curry favor of them. When the U.S. government withdrew from UNESCO, most Americans condoned the action.

With the United Nations believed to be drifting toward the organizational graveyard where the League of Nations is buried, and established national and local institutions failing, many men and women - even children - developed a callous "me first" attitude, expending most of their energy to coping with the hopelessness gripping humanity. What made matters worse was that no one of note, no one we respected - not a single reputable institution - expressed optimism regarding the future. All of the geopolitical pundits - in the East and West - saw only a long, protracted, painful struggle ahead for humankind. The greatest deterrent to war, they felt, was for each side to add to its military might. Respect for each others' power, they believed, would keep each side from striking first. Their advice was heeded by governmental leaders who knew more about preparing for war - than peace.

In fact, throughout the '70s and '80s the think-tank analysts were suspicious of any talk of peace. Having lived through World War Two, the Korean war, the Vietnam War, and having wrestled daily with the problems emerging from the Cold War, they developed the opinion that

26

global peace was a pipe dream. All they could offer their countrymen, in the way of advice, was: Learn to adapt, as best as possible, to the ongoing struggle whose end was precariously uncertain.

Many of us who were buckling under the Cold War pressure sought immediate relief, looking in every direction. We searched for a savior, someone who could help us forget our personal problems and society's insurmountable deficiencies; someone who could provide us with comfort during - what seemed like - unbearable times; someone who could assure us that everything was going to be "okay."

In America, President Ronald Reagan exploited those yearnings by crafting a glowing image of America. By telling us that we were great, by branding as doomsayers those social observers who were critical of America's social condition he painted a glorious picture of our country's destiny. Most Americans hailed him as a savior. Because of him, we sang the national anthem with gusto and celebrated Independence Day with pride. Displaying and waving the American flag became a passion. The nationalistic fervor whipped up by President Reagan created a state of euphoria within most elements in the country. It was the kind of high one experiences from morphine. In a drug-induced state, all thoughts are focused on one's good feelings; and there's the gnawing need to experience those feelings more and more. President Reagan's administration was accommodating.

For the majority of people in America, President Reagan's international and domestic policies were working well. He was able to win the release of the U.S. diplomats being held hostage in Iran. His "get tough" policy toward international terrorism was popular. Most Americans' national pride swelled when he had Libya bombed for terrorist acts directed against U.S. soldiers in Germany. And when he ordered the military overthrow of the Marxist regime in Grenada , many Americans' faith in their country received a big boost.

Ending the military draft made him popular with the youth. His free trade policy won favor with the internationalists and business community. High defense spending created more jobs than ever before. The American economy was booming. During his presidency inflation was slashed substantially. So were the interest rates on bank loans. The morale of the armed forces was lifted, and he was able to closet the ghost of Vietnam, which had haunted Americans for years. Through his charisma, President

Reagan was able to restore confidence in the nation's institutions. He became the first president in nearly two decades to serve two full terms. But there was a downside to Reagan's tenure as president.

While most Americans basked in the sunlight of a revised patriotism based on a romanticized view of the nation's past, the social problems that plagued the country prior to President Reagan's ascendancy were neglected. Racism worsened, environmental pollution reached the hazardous point, AIDS became an epidemic, drug use appeared uncontrollable, spreading to all strata of society, the underclass evolved into a ticking time-bomb, homelessness mounted, the United States became the largest debtor nation in the world.

What made this brief period in recent American history surreal was the fact that those who cheered the loudest knew deep down that they were being fooled. The threat of a nuclear holocaust remained a persistent subconscious fear, which would surface into the conscious mind whenever President Reagan's reference to the Soviet Union as an "evil empire" was recalled. However, the Reagan administration was adroit in turning such proclamations into a vehicle that would heighten the people's already growing patriotism - and strengthen the president's followers' allegiance to him. It didn't matter that the catalytic agent was hate. The majority of Americans went along with this kind of mind control, because they felt that it was better to allow themselves to be fooled and feel good than be depressed while waiting for the ballistic missile to strike.

5

The End of the Two Sides

The ballistic missile never struck. In fact, what was least expected happened. In early 1990 the Cold War ended. It ended in a way none of us - not even the eminent Cold War strategists - expected. It happened so fast, it took some time for us to adjust to the idea. While watching it unfold on television, we couldn't believe what we were witnessing. It was like watching a prime time drama; when we turned off the television set, our Cold War fears were still intact.

Our skepticism was based on 40 years of having to endure the Cold War, 40 years of girding ourselves for the unthinkable to occur, 40 years of repressing fears, 40 years of trying to evade the grasp of doom.

We couldn't instantaneously strip ourselves of feelings that had been ingrained in our consciousness. A weaning process was necessary. The more we read about the Cold War ending and the more we talked about it, the more we gravitated toward acceptance, and a sense of hope began to percolate within us. It wasn't a case of being swept up in a state of exaltation, although there were moments when we felt like jumping for joy; but when that feeling would suddenly seize us, the undercurrent of doubt that was still very much a part of us restrained us.

It was fascinating watching the expressions on the faces of television newscasters reporting daily the unraveling of the Soviet empire in Eastern Europe. It was as if they were reporting miracles. Having been a journalist on a network level, I knew how they felt. For years they had reported the

Cold War machinations and intrigues and the bitterness and suspicion that had been generated in the East and West. We were all dumbfounded, even the pundits in Washington and academic centers that had been following Cold War developments for decades. Practically overnight the Cold War strategies stored in Harvard University's School of Government computers were obsolete. We found ourselves fumbling with the idea of peace. In a way, it was like having to deal with a distant dream come true. We were unprepared to build and manage a peaceful world. We were conditioned to flinch or duck and shoot, and not welcome a stranger with open arms. We were suspect of all utopianists. But it wasn't only that that prevented us from focusing on peace. We wanted to know how the Cold War ended. Without that knowledge, we thought, it would be difficult to concentrate on finding the right way to establish peace, for somehow, knowing how the Cold War ended would convince us that it really ended, that we hadn't been fooled.

There were wild guesses, educated guesses, all sorts of theories propounded - some reasonable and others irrational. But the wisest among the theorists admitted that they were mystified. Considering the magnitude of the event, I - and many others - could appreciate the editors of a famous British newspapers' assessment. They attributed the cessation of the Cold War to the intervention of an "Invisible Hand."

While many of us could accept that explanation, we still felt that there had to have been signs that the Berlin Wall would be torn down; that the barbed wire fence between Hungary and Austria would be cut down; that Poland, Hungary, East Germany, Czechoslovakia, Bulgaria and Romania would shed themselves of Communist control and embrace democracy; that even Albania would break out of its self imposed isolation, reaching out earnestly for international relations; that the Soviet Union would openly acknowledge its economic and political shortcomings and conscientiously pursue reforms that would make for a more democratic government and freer society; that republics within the Soviet Union would openly declare their independence; that the Russians would not stand in the way of German reunification; that religious freedom would be granted to all Soviet citizens; and, finally, that the Soviet Union would dissolve.

There seemed to be a powerful urge among oppressed people everywhere to fight for their freedom. A grassroots rebellion in Nepal forced its absolute monarch to relinquish his power for a parliamentary form of government; the white rulers of South Africa suddenly decided to free the original African National Congress leadership, including Nelson Mandela, and begin serious negotiations to change the political structure of the nation. Racist South West Africa, a long-time protectorate of the Union of South Africa, became a democratic independent black-ruled nation, called Namibia. The Soviet Union and the United States worked together in helping Namibia come into being. The Angola civil war ended - again, through the help of a joint Moscow-Washington effort. Nicaragua's dictator agreed to free elections, which resulted in his ouster and the formation of a multiparty democracy; nations of Asia and Africa made commitments to democratic elections.

If there had been signs of what eventually unfolded we didn't notice them, because when you are consumed by doubts and fear and afflicted by pain, you are so preoccupied with your personal suffering that you're not motivated to look for hopeful signs. That's why it took some time before most of us could accept the reality of there being no more Cold War, and perhaps why it will take even longer to fully appreciate what has happened in the world. Nevertheless, during this period of uncertainty we marveled and cheered as we watched men and women hammer down the Berlin Wall, releasing feelings they never dreamed of being able to release. Though thousands of miles away, I wept along with them as I watched their dance of freedom on television. It was a historic event because it marked the beginning of a new era, in which more and more people - high and low - realized the futility, the utter absurdity of constantly preparing for war.

National enemies started talking to each other. After 40 years of hostility, the South Korean and North Korean prime ministers met, setting the stage for unification talks. The urge to cooperate seemed to be replacing the need to compete: companies from different countries were pooling their resources to produce common products. The Japanese and Americans were building cars together, as well as airplanes; the Russians and Germans were involved in joint ventures. United States publishers were editing and designing books and printing them in South Korea and Hong Kong. The Japanese were setting up manufacturing plants in America and employing Americans. In Taiwan, U.S. companies were establishing plants and hiring Taiwanese. Many other countries were involved in this kind of economic cross pollination.

There was a collective desire to undo the sins of the past. The Soviet Union admitted that it - and not the Nazis - slaughtered thousands of Polish Army officers at the Katyn Forest near Smolensk in the early 1940s; East Germany publicly acknowledged its citizens' role in the Holocaust and asked for forgiveness of the Jews - and established diplomatic relations with Israel. This compulsion to share the truth led to the exposure of political and economic corruption in countries throughout the world. Governments in South Korea and Japan fell because of unethical behavior; the Speaker of the U.S. House of Representatives was forced to resign; there were mass purges of corrupt officials in the Soviet Union; and, ultimately, the demise of the very nation which the United States battled in the Cold War.

It was also a time when 12 Western European countries agreed to unite politically, as well as economically - with the Eastern Europeans expressing a desire to join the compact, and the Soviet Union making overtures about joining. In Southeast Asia, Malaysia, the Philippines, Singapore, Thailand and Indonesia were making plans to organize a common market. Most Caribbean nations formed an economic union. Australia and New Zealand signed a free-trade agreement; the United States and Canada did likewise, with Mexico planning to join them. The free trade relationship being created by Argentina and Brazil was viewed as the first step in the development of a South American common market.

National isolationism was dead. It was obvious that every country was dependent on another country for something. Even the superpowers and industrial giants required resources and technological know-how from other countries in order to maintain their position in the world. The tariff barrier was becoming an economic fossil. Many economists recognized that nations were functioning in a global economy. While the evidence of international economic, social and political cooperation was mounting, and the momentum toward world unity was quickening, not everyone relished the changes that were taking place.

There was some stiff resistance. In what was still the Soviet Union, for example, a well-organized opposition toward "perestroika" emerged. In the United States, labor unions waged an anti international trade campaign, which urged Americans to buy only American made products. And there was growing resentment against foreign firms purchasing U.S. firms and real estate. The democratic advancements in China seemed to

32

come to an end when its political leadership employed military might to crush a prolonged pro democracy rally in Tiananmen Square. Anti-Arab and anti-Jewish sentiment was growing in France. Neo-Nazi elements were emerging in Germany. The skinheads were winning recruits in America and Britain.

Fear fueled the resistance movements. There was the fear of the unknown, which seemed to be the biggest obstacle. Some people preferred the status quo, reasoning that at least it is something that was familiar; something new might result in greater hardships. The fear of uniformity and over centralization caused some to feel that humans would turn into robots and cultural diversity would disappear. Others felt that world unity would lead to a loss of freedom, the establishment of a global dictatorship. And fundamentalist religionists wailed that the movement toward internationalism was a sign that the Antichrist was among us.

Yet, despite the fear and skepticism in some quarters, and despite the forceful militant opposition that erupted in violence at times, the movement toward international cooperation and unity went on unabated; in fact, it began to accelerate, with a speed that made many of us wonder what was propelling us in an unfamiliar direction. Some of us sensed an extraordinary force had to be clearing the way and drawing us forward to a glorious time, long awaited.

More and more people were beginning to realize that the planet Earth was really our home, and the house, town and country we lived in were simply aspects of that home. Because nations shared similar problems, they consulted together to find solutions. They realized that air and water pollution and drug trafficking were no respectors of national boundaries. Colombia, Bolivia, Peru and the United States banded together to try to wipe out the drug trade in the Western Hemisphere. To prevent the extinction of the elephant, African, European and Asian nations hammered out a pact that would put an end to producing ivory products made from elephant tusks. International treaties were forged to curb whale hunting and keep tuna fishermen from snaring dolphins; treaties limiting ocean garbage disposal were also drafted; and nations around the world pooled their resources to thwart airline terrorism. The Soviet Union and other Eastern European countries joined Interpol - an international police force.

A surge of altruism and neighborly good will was infused into the world. Disasters in one country brought relief from other countries.

Famine in Ethiopia and the Sudan drew help from scores of nations - from as far away as Japan and Canada; and when an earthquake devastated a section of Soviet Armenia, killing thousands of men, women and children, food, medical supplies and skilled rescue workers were flown in to alleviate the suffering. It was as if we were beginning to gain an inkling of the reality of the oneness of the human family. More and more people - on all continents - started to think and talk about the possibility of the establishment of a world government.

6

On the Threshold of Peace

I no longer had to hide from my intellectual friends the belief that by the end of this century the nations of the world would be drawn together - and there would be no more global strife. In fact, I openly shared that view; and the responses ranged from a cautious, "It seems possible," to an enthusiastic, "Yes, we're headed in that direction." What was refreshing was that no one belittled the idea of peace by the year 2000. And a few close friends to whom I had confided years ago reminded me, when the Berlin Wall started coming down, that they hadn't forgotten what I had shared with them during the dark days of the Cold War. They looked upon me as some sort of seer.

Of course I'm not a seer - and told them so, even shared with them my secret struggle to prevent my doubts from shattering my faith. I must admit that the remarkable events from late 1989 to early 1990 not only bolstered my faith - they moved me to explore from a Baha'i perspective the signs that led to the sudden geopolitical realignments that sparked in people everywhere a hope in the future that months before seemed impossible. The thought of engaging in the exploration was both frightening and exhilarating. It was frightening because I doubted my ability to carry out the mission successfully, since even the most erudite international relations authorities were stunned by the abrupt end of the Cold War and the demise of communism as a powerful political and economic force in the world.

On the other hand, part of me looked forward to the undertaking of putting together what was to become a most extraordinary puzzle. One thing I was sure of: whatever I discovered would be linked to the "Invisible Hand," the one that leading newspaper credited with creating the unbelievable transformation in Eastern Europe and the rest of the world.

In a way you can liken the dramatic change in world affairs and people's outlook to the development of a majestic tree from scratch. The early stages of growth aren't discernible to the naked eye. When it breaks through the ground, it attracts little or no attention, for it is fragile and slight. It takes time before its trunk is sturdy, and its branches are fully mature, and its roots are sufficiently spread to sources of nourishment. During most of its growth the tree isn't appreciated; however, when it finally unfolds to its destined grandeur, it is as if it popped into being instantaneously.

One could argue that today's dramatic changes can be traced to the emergence of man millions of years ago, just as you can trace an apple's origin to the seed of the tree that produced it. Prior to the Industrial Revolution changes in all phases of life seemed to occur so slowly they were hardly discernible. For thousands of years man's means of communication and transportation remained virtually the same. So did the way communities were ruled.

But in the early 1800s change started to occur in dramatic fashion. In the past 190 years, 95 percent of all inventions have occurred; and with each passing year the quantity and quality of invention has improved. It has been during this period that mankind has made its greatest progress toward maturity. Events occurred - some mystical in nature - that propelled humanity to the threshold of world peace. While the changes were occurring, people in the 19th and for the most part 20th centuries weren't aware of why the changes were taking place and what they would lead to. Very few people knew that the "Invisible Hand" was pointing the way. They had no idea there would be something like the Cold War, with its unspeakable dangers haunting and terrorizing humans everywhere. Even the most powerful couldn't stem the gales of change.

The handful of mighty European rulers, meeting at the Congress of Vienna in 1815 to establish, once and for all, their indisputable dominance on the Continent, had absolutely no inkling of the monumental, transformative process that would soon be launched, defusing, in time, their invincibility, and leading an unsuspecting humanity into the era of internationalism - an essential step in the fulfillment of the promise inherent in the Lord's Prayer.

At the time, Britain, France, Prussia, Russia and Austria maintained the mightiest military forces in the world, used for, among other things, empire-building enterprises believed to be divinely sanctioned. No other nation dared to challenge their assumption. It appeared that these rulers were destined to carve up the rest of the world and rule forever, prepared to crush the slightest sign of grassroots democratic activity. In the meantime, their subjects - the masses - remained resigned to a pitiful fate of continuous struggle for survival.

But the perfectly plotted plan didn't work - despite the efforts of cunning and brilliant geopolitical strategists like Prince von Metternich. Bickering between the superpowers of the day exploded into warfare. By the mid-1800s many people were fed up with the bloodshed, the greed and corruption of their rulers, and the inordinate taxes. Some of the disenfranchised grew restless, wanting changes. Underground protest groups formed. New political and economic ideologies developed, which exploited the dissatisfaction of the masses. The followers and sympathizers took to the streets, demanding greater social and economic justice, as well as political freedom. And Karl Marx and Friedrich Engels were hammering out a solution to what they believed was the "spectre haunting Europe."

Socialism caught the imagination of the downtrodden and some idealists, scaring the aristocratic and mercantile classes, and sparking an ongoing struggle between leftist and rightist ideologues and the have and have-nots. Through the years the struggle would take on many forms, and bring about many social, economic and political changes that none of the 19th century social theorists foresaw. During the beginning of this period of political and social upheaval, the map of Europe began to change. Prussia persuaded most of the nearby German-speaking principalities to form the nation of Germany. Despite vigorous papal opposition, including military force, a courageous populist campaign seized all of the Papal States and formed the Italian nation. European royalty was undergoing changes. Constitutional monarchy was replacing absolute monarchism. Some audacious social activists dared to challenge the immovable establishment, which, surprisingly, gave in to an extent. Progress created a popular clamor for more reform. Britain abolished slavery; America did the same. Russia outlawed serfdom. Bismarck instigated a social security scheme for all German citizens - and offered full citizenship to the Jews. There were successful drives to improve conditions in mental hospitals and prisons in America and Europe. Child labor was being exposed as a social abuse, prompting legislative action in a number of countries. Temperance societies flourished in the 1840s in America. A few courageous women trumpeted a call for equal status with men. In the West, the brilliant Margaret Fuller, America's first feminist, equated the treatment of women with slavery. Her persistent and powerful pleas for equality inspired the first women's rights convention in 1848. In the East, a Persian poetess, Tahirih, championed woman's rights in a society that viewed women as sub-humans devoid of souls. Despite threats on her life, she openly called for the emancipation of women. Even a few sympathetic men found her bold approach too much to bear. When she removed her veil at a conference of social and spiritual reformers in Badasht, many men fled the room. One slit his throat. The story of Tahirih's struggle and martyrdom spread to Europe, inspiring women there to take up the feminist cause.

A great wave of expectancy swept over Europe, North America and the Middle East in the mid-1800s, even among people who had no idea of what exactly was in store for them - and for future generations. Something wonderful was anticipated. It was in the air, even in the hearts of men and women who were once enveloped by despair. There was talk of world peace, of world brotherhood, of the coming of paradise on Earth. Utopian communities sprang up, trying hard to create the perfect life. Noted philosophers and writers like Thomas Carlyle and Matthew Arnold turned into visionaries, expressing faith in humanity's brilliant destiny. German Jean Paul Friedrich Richter was one of the many positive prognosticators among the romantic period writers of the day: "But there will come another era ... when it shall be light, and man will awaken from his lofty dreams, and find - his dreams still there, and that nothing is gone save his sleep ... Infinite Providence, Thou wilt cause the day to dawn."

Poets like Alfred Tennyson sensed that a new era was dawning:
The old order changeth, yielding place to new,
And God fulfills Himself in many ways,
Lest one good custom should corrupt the world.
Tennyson also sensed that the new world order he envisioned wouldn't

emerge easily:

Ring out old shapes of foul disease;
Ring out the narrowing lust of gold;
Ring out the thousand wars of old,
Ring in the thousand years of peace.

Ring in the valiant man and free,
The larger heart, the kindlier hand;
Ring out the darkness of the land,
Ring in the Christ that is to be.

In America, "The Battle Hymn of the Republic" was being sung with a passion that springs from a deep faith and love. In churches, schools, in club rooms and granary halls, in theaters across the land the verse, "Mine eyes hath seen the coming of the glory of the Lord," rang out like a fervent prayer. It was a time of bold thinking - and major philosophical and scientific breakthroughs, some seriously challenging established religious dogma that had imprisoned minds for centuries.

Two scientists, Britishers Charles Darwin and A.R. Wallace, forged, around the same time, similar theories regarding the origin and development of humankind. Neither had been aware of what the other had been doing. Was it sheer coincidence that two men living independently would conceive a theory that would revolutionize humanity's understanding of its development as a species? Or was it the "Invisible Hand" coming to rescue humanity once again from blunders born of arrogance and ignorance ?

As scientists began to embrace the Theory of Evolution, an avalanche of invention followed - over a 150-year period - that made instantaneous communications between people in different hemispheres possible, that took humans to the moon and beyond, that extended man's longevity and turned former headhunters into computer programmers.

In the mid-1800s the atmosphere among the learned was charged with a need for change and a hunger for scientific exploration and technological creativity. Famous artist Samuel F.B. Morse gave up painting to invent the telegraph. On May 24, 1844, the first telegraphic message was sent from Washington to Baltimore, expressing the spirit of the day. The message - "What Hath God Wrought!" - was selected from the Bible.

The phenomenal interest in science was matched by a similar interest in religion. At times the two clashed. Especially when the Theory of Evolution gained popularity. Some leading religionists branded the theory as the work of the devil, designed to purge the truth from minds of scientists, theologians and laymen. In America and Europe, churches were plagued with discord and conflict. The Methodists, Baptists and Presbyterians splintered over the slavery issue. There was a call for religious reform, some of it so passionate it was viewed as revolutionary, even heretical. The Danish philosopher/theologian Soren Kierkegaard, in his "Attack on Christendom," chastised clergymen for wasting their time arguing over meaningless questions like, "How many angels dance on the point of a pin?" He exhorted his fellow clerics to spend their time lifting the masses from the much of superstition and ignorance - as Jesus did. Kierkegaard's views won wide acclaim among the non-religious, and - predictably - scorn from the religious establishment.

Overshadowing the campaigns for church reform, however, was the millennial fervor spanning three continents. In America, Charles Finney, lawyer-turned-evangelist, mesmerized huge crowds with his powerful logic and vivid description of hell. "If the church," he would roar, "will do her duty, the millennium may come to this country in three years."

Thousands of devout Christians felt that Christ's return was imminent. Respected seers, as well as unknowns, reported visions and powerful dreams of Jesus back on Earth - preaching and healing. Popular Adventist movements resulted from these revelations. Mormonism, The Seventh-day Adventist Church and spiritualism sprang up around this time. The Shakers' popularity was peaking. Most of these religious communities - and others - were awaiting the year 1844 with great anticipation. A number of biblical scholars like William Miller of Western Massachusetts calculated independently, from references in the Bible, that Jesus would return around 1844. Followers of Miller and other Adventists flocked to the mountains of Pennsylvania and Western Massachusetts to gaze at the sky to look for Jesus descending on a cloud.

The great arrival turned out to be a great disappointment. Jesus didn't come as the Adventists expected. After several minor arrival time extensions, most Adventists abandoned their belief that Christ would return in body. Yet, they still believed their biblical calculations were correct; something spiritually stupendous would occur around 1844, a year some religionists were calling the "Year of the Lord." In reviewing their evidence, many felt that God had not forsaken them, that they had simply misunderstood the biblical signs, and that He had, indeed, intervened, infusing into the world the Spirit of Christ. But some didn't give up their "Second Coming" belief and continued to scan the sky. The Roman Catholic monks in a monastery on Mount Carmel continued to search the heavens.

In the mid-1800s German biblical scholar Leonard H. Kelber searched the Christian scripture for clues as to Christ's return. After an exhaustive study, he was convinced that the second coming would take place on Mount Carmel (the Mountain of God) in what is now Haifa, Israel.

Kelber and his followers left their jobs, sold their property and sailed for the Holy Land. They set up a colony at the foot of Mount Carmel, chiseling over their doorways, in German, the words "Der Herr Ist Nahe" (The Lord is near). And they waited. One generation after another waited until most of the descendants of the first arrivals were arrested as Nazi collaborators and deported to internment camps in South Africa.

In North America, many American Indian tribes were awaiting the coming of a Messiah that would unite all of the world's tribes. The coming of a great prophet that would bring a new religion is part of the Hopi tradition. The new religion would call for the establishment of one language for the world, an end to all war and violence, an end to the destruction and exploitation of the Earth by humans and the union and understanding between all races. It would be a religion that would have its beginning in three great central figures. The great holy man, Black Elk, of the Oglala Sioux, saw in his visions the coming of a great man from the east with long flowing hair, but was neither white nor an Indian in appearance. Black Elk saw that when people embraced this new message, they would become ablaze with it, spreading it to other people. But those who didn't see the new message would grope blindly on earth.

Halfway across the world, in India, the education commissioner of Indore State, G. S. Arundale, had been touched by the great wave of expectation that was sweeping the planet. In his book, "The Coming World Teacher," he wrote: "So many thousands of people all over the world believe in the near coming of a Great World Teacher that the existence of this belief is a matter of common knowledge, at least among the educated people."

Among the Jews there was a sign of hope that there might be a chance of returning to the Holy Land soon. Getting back was a dream that haunted them for centuries, ever since the Diaspora. Jews prayed that God would find a way of opening the gates of Israel. Generation after generation prayed. But the gates remained closed ever since the Christian and Muslim leadership in the Holy Land agreed hundreds of years earlier to bar Jewish entry. To those Jews who had successfully assimilated into the secular cultures of lands where they resided, returning to Israel seemed impossible. Wresting the Holy Land away from the Ottoman Empire was out of the question. Even the mighty British Empire wouldn't dare try.

So financial tycoons like the Rothschilds devised an alternative scheme: They planned to purchase what is today Uganda, Africa, and turn it into a Jewish homeland. But that plan was never carried out. In 1844, the Edict of Toleration was signed, revoking the ancient pact barring Jewish resettlement in Israel. The gates were opened a bit, the Turks allowing only a few Jews to enter at a time. But it took time to spread the good news to the Jewish communities scattered over Europe, North Africa and the Near East. When many of the rabbis received the message, they reacted skeptically, for they believed that the Messiah had to be in the Holy Land before a Jewish homeland could be established. For the most part, non-religious Jews made the long trek to the "Promised Land" determined to turn the desert into a rose garden. Theodor Herzl, the founder of Zionism, proclaimed that the "Messianic Spirit" was back in the world. Though the state of Israel exists today, thousands of Jews living there refuse to recognize it, clinging to the belief that the Messiah would have to be in the Holy Land before a Jewish homeland could be created. Some Israelis wonder silently: "Did He come - and we missed Him?"

There were millenarian stirrings in the Moslem world also. Some highly respected mystics and scholars of the Koran were expecting two messianic figures to arise before the resurrection day. First, the Mahdi (rightly-guided one) would appear, sent by the Prophet Muhammad to establish justice in a world filled with inequity. Then, they felt, Jesus Christ would return. Many Moslem theologians wondered when the great advent would occur. Based on their study of the Koran and Islamic traditions, members of the Shaykhi group of scholars and students, believed the Mahdi would reveal Himself in 1844, somewhere in or around Iran. Shaykhis scoured the region seeking the "Promised One."

7
Age of Enlightenment

On May 23, 1844, a new religion was born. Sayyid Ali Muhammad, a young merchant of Shiraz, Iran, revealed himself to a Shaykhi follower as the One who was being sought. He took the title Bab, meaning gate. After him, he prophesied, another prophet would appear whose major mission would be to provide the impetus and guidance for the establishment of world peace.

Within 40 days, 17 others, from all parts of Iran and generally unaware of each other, recognized the Bab's claim. Among these disciples was Tahirih, the brilliant poet and fighter for women's rights.

The Bab produced a new holy book (The Bayan), abrogating the Koran. While his progressive teachings upset most of the Shiite Muslim clergy, by 1849 about 100,000 Iranians embraced the new faith. A wave of persecution was set off by the clergy - but the Babis fought back. The fighting grew so intense that the shah dispatched troops to quell the unrest. After being officially proclaimed a heretic, the Bab was executed, and his followers hounded. The unusual circumstances surrounding his execution stunned those who witnessed it and aroused the curiosity of those who heard about it from eyewitnesses. His execution by firing squad took place on July 9, 1850, in Tabriz. More than 10,000 people gathered on the rooftops overlooking the barracks square, the site of the execution. In his cell in the barracks which served as his final prison, the Bab was talking confidentially to his secretary when the executioner arrived to fetch him.

The Bab turned to him and said, "Not until I have said to him all those things that I wish to say can any earthly power silence me. Though all the world be armed against me, yet shall it be powerless to deter me from fulfilling, to the last word, my intention." To the firing squad leader, an Armenian Christian who didn't want to carry out his orders for fear of provoking the wrath of God, the Bab gave this assurance: "Follow your instructions, and if your intention be sincere, the Almighty is surely able to relieve you of your perplexity."

The Bab and a youth who had begged to be martyred with him were hung by ropes from a spike driven into a column in the square, and faced a firing squad of 750 soldiers. The Armenian officer gave the command to fire. When the smoke cleared, the spectators couldn't believe what had happened. The Bab was nowhere in sight and the youth was standing alive and unhurt before them! The ropes that had held them had merely been severed by the volley. A frenzied search ensued. The Bab was finally found in his cell, finishing his talk with his secretary. As the executioners approached he told them, "I have finished my conversation ... Now you may proceed to fulfill your intention." The original executioner and firing squad leader refused to participate in any further attempts to harm the Bab, but others readily volunteered to replace him.

On the second attempt the bullets tore into the bodies of the 31-year-old prophet and his young companion. Before the order to fire was issued, the Bab addressed these words to the thousands of onlookers: "O wayward generation! Had you believed in me every one of you would have followed the example of this youth, who stood in rank above most of you, and would have willingly sacrificed himself in my path. The day will come when you will have recognized me; that day I shall have ceased to be with you." As the shots were fired, a violent gale swept over Tabriz, setting off a blinding whirlwind of dust that plunged the city in darkness from noon until evening. In Shiraz an earthquake rocked the city, causing panic among its inhabitants. The devastation was such that an epidemic of cholera broke out and famine followed.

A foiled attempt by a few disturbed, revenge-seeking Babis to kill the shah infuriated the government. A nationwide witch-hunt for Babis was launched, which led to the torture and mass killings of thousands of men, women and children. News of the shah's ferocious persecution of the Babis reached the West. French historian Ernest Renan witnessed the sadistic butchery of hundreds of Babis in a single day in the streets of Tehran. He called the experience "a day perhaps unparalleled in the history of the world."

Another European eyewitness, an Austrian, Captain Von Goumoens, wrote to his fellow countrymen, "... Would to God that I had not lived to see it! But by the duties of my profession I was unhappily often, only too often, a witness of these abominations." French historian Count de Gobineau immortalized the struggle of the Babis by describing their steadfast adherence to truth; of self denial; of sacrifice; of joyful constancy in the face of torture and death.

Years later the dramatic story of the Bab and his followers inspired some European writers to create poems about the martyred prophet. A play was written and performed throughout Europe. The Bab's liberal teachings also caught the attention of some Western scholars and journalists. Cambridge University orientalist Edward G. Browne wrote that the Bab's teachings "appealed most strongly to those - and they are numerous in Persia - who were filled with longings for freedom from iron dogma, and for a more humane social order."

Writing in the magazine "Hours at Home," E. P. Evans revealed that he found it remarkable that the Babi faith attracted followers "not merely from the poor and ignorant populace, but chiefly from the highest and most intelligent classes of society, priests, philosophers, nobles, men of wealth and education; and that nevertheless, Christendom should have remained almost as ignorant of this great event as if it had taken place in the moon or the inhabitants of another planet."

In her "Story of the Bab," Mary F. Wilson likened the sufferings of the Bab and his followers to the sufferings of Jesus and his followers. She also expressed admiration for the Bab's teachings: "Some of those innovations were probably the result of his study of European books. But the considerate kindness of all his rules for women , and his invariable tenderness in everything that concerned children, must have had a deeper source."

To most of the Babis, Christ's return did follow the Mahdi's appearance. Thirteen years following the Bab's execution, an Iranian nobleman, Mirza Husayn Ali (titled Baha'u'llah, or the Glory of God), revealed to a few relatives and friends in Baghdad, where he had been exiled for his Babi beliefs, that he was the One whom the Bab had promised would come to provide the guidance needed to unite humankind and establish world peace. Most of the Babis were thrilled with the news of Baha'u'llah's announcement, for they had been virtually leaderless since the Bab's execution, and were falling into disarray. Though exiled in neighboring Ottoman Iraq, Baha'u'llah managed to send emissaries to Iran to spread the word among the Babis - and unite them. In a relatively short period of time, most of them became ardent Baha'is or followers of Baha'u'llah.

Professor Browne, the only Western scholar to interview Baha'u'llah, gained some understanding as to why the Babis viewed Baha'u'llah as the return of Christ: "The face of him on whom I gazed I can never forget, though I cannot describe it. Those piercing eyes seemed to read one's very soul; power and authority sat on that ample brow; while the deep lines on the forehead and face implied an age which the jet-black hair and beard flowing down in indistinguishable luxuriance almost to the waist seemed to belie. No need to ask in whose presence I stood, as I bowed myself before One who is the object of a devotion and love which kings might envy and emperors sigh in vain!"

Baha'u'llah was repulsed by violence, and concerned about the plight of the poor. His vision was universal - far greater than that of the repressive political and religious leaders of his homeland. He viewed the world as "one country and mankind its citizens," calling upon all rulers to gather for the purpose of devising the means of ending war and establishing global peace through the formation of a federal world government. Should any state attack another, he said, all others must combine to stop the aggressor. He advocated the establishment of a world language and script; a world economy and monetary system. Viewing religious and ethnic prejudice as the major cause of human disunity, Baha'u'llah appealed to all to strive for unity through love of one's fellow man. In this connection, he abrogated the Islamic and Babi principle of holy war (Jihad), proclaiming it is better to be killed than to kill.

Shortly before being banished for life to the fortress prison in Acre, Palestine, Baha'u'llah started sending epistles to the kings and rulers of the world, including Queen Victoria, Napoleon III, the Ottoman sultan, the Iranian shah, Russia's tsar, Germany's kaiser, and Pope Pius IX. In his messages, he clearly described his messianic station and mission, urging them to heed his counsel. Had the rulers accepted his message, Baha'u'llah declared, "The Most Great Peace" would have been established on earth.

Instead, he predicted, a "Lesser Peace" would eventually be forged, but not without much travail and sorrow. That peace would spring from a desperation felt everywhere on the planet. Nations, out of necessity, would band together politically and economically. Baha'u'llah provided his followers with a glimpse of the process that would lead to the lesser peace, declaring, "The world's equilibrium hath been upset through the vibrating influence of this most great, this new World Order. Mankind's ordered life hath been revolutionized through the agency of this unique, this wondrous System - like of which mortal eyes have never witnessed." "The Hand of Omnipotence hath established His revelation upon an unassailable, an enduring foundation. Storms of human strife are powerless to undermine its basis, nor will men's fanciful theories succeed in damaging its structure." "The day is approaching when we will have rolled up the world and all that is therein, and spread out a new world order."

The new world order that Baha'u'llah envisioned would be the final stage of man's social evolution, having experienced the family, clan, tribal, city-state and independent sovereign nation stages - and all the agonizing growing pains along the way. In the last stage, humankind would be united, participating as world citizens in a planetary civilization that would demonstrate a genuine appreciation for the rich diversity in the human family. Though no world renowned political leader or religious potentate accepted Baha'u'llah's claim, the two highest ranking men in the Acre area were drawn to him. The Muslim caliph and Turkish governor came regularly to his jail cell, seeking advice and counsel. The cleric became a Baha'i; and the governor became an admirer who pleaded with Baha'u'llah to move out of the prison - and live anywhere he wished in the the Acre-Haifa area.

During a self-imposed period of house arrest, Baha'u'llah revealed his most important book, the Kitabi Aqdas (The Book of Laws). Finally persuaded by his eldest son and the governor to venture out of the house, Baha'u'llah journeyed four times to Haifa, one time finding lodging in one of the homes built by Kelber's followers. On his last visit, he climbed Mount Carmel, entered the Cave of Elijah and in a booming voice proclaimed who he was: "Call out to Zion, O Carmel, and announce the joyful tidings: He that was hidden from mortal eyes is come! His all conquering sovereignty is manifest; His all encompassing splendor is revealed ...". When Baha'u'llah died in 1892, his successor, Abdul Baha, himself not a prophet of God, carried his father's message of unity and peace to Europe and America, sharing it with the famous as well as the downtrodden. Wherever he went, he was hailed as a messenger of peace. Press coverage was extensive. His views - always a reflection of his father's teachings - helped lift audiences' vision to possibilities never before considered. He called the 20th century "a century of light," an unprecedented time when the nations of the world would unite and justice would reign. This, despite his repeated warnings of impending danger facing humanity. Abdul Baha foresaw World War One; and while the League of Nations was forming, predicted its downfall - and World War Two. Communism, he stated, would gain great popularity, especially among the underdeveloped nations and oppressed peoples, but in time would evaporate. Without a divine consciousness, he pointed out, a society is cut off from divine assistance and devolves into ruin.

The Baha'i Faith has evolved into a world religion, with its international headquarters on Mount Carmel, and its 5 million adherents spread over 111,000 localities around the globe. Since the early 1800s tremendous progress has been made on all fronts. Humanity seems to be pulling together; in part through incredible advancements in communications and transportation technology. For centuries humans relied on pigeons, drums and horse-delivered letters to send messages. From 1844 to the present, communications has evolved from the telegraph to the communications satellite; and, transportation from steam ships to space ships. Socially, women have made great strides in gaining equal status with men; there's greater labor-management harmony; an international economy has emerged; ancient deadly diseases have been conquered; more people than ever before have access to education; old social abuses like wife beating and child abuse are being addressed; long-lingering and festering prejudices are being openly challenged, and in some instances being overcome by individual initiative and community effort; knowledge is replacing superstition. Nations that were once bitter enemies are being drawn together to form powerful economic and political unions.

During this relatively short period of time, humans have been able to see the planet we live on as it is seen from outer space, forcing us to expand our awareness of reality and question what we wouldn't have dared question in the past. This experience - and science's major breakthroughs in understanding the nature of life - has expanded our vision of reality. We see things now we didn't see before. Many scientists now recognize that everything is interrelated and continuously changing, that space and time are not separate, that the material and spiritual worlds are intertwined, essentially one in the same, and that what we perceive as truth is actually an approximation of reality. They have scrapped the long-held notion that the universe operates like a great big machine, realizing now that it functions more like a dynamic web of interwoven relationships; that it is, in essence, a colossal dramatic event, with every human being, every animal, every plant, every rock, every drop in the ocean, connected aspects of it.

The discovery of the principle of the interrelatedness of nature has spawned other discoveries. We now realize that the whole determines the behavior of its parts, and not the other way around, which for centuries was held as a fundamental truth. We also recognize that the linear view of the world, propounded by the great mechanistic thinkers of the past, is flawed. Ours is a non-linear world, where a small force or cause can, under the right conditions, lead to a vast effect. This is true in both the spiritual and material realms. Some scientists are seriously exploring a frontier that many scientists in the past claimed didn't exist - namely, what mystics and religionists call "the hereafter." Considerable evidence is being compiled to support the belief that it does exist.

It would be difficult for any rational person to deny that, since the Congress of Vienna made its mission clear, what has occurred has been stupendous. An unprecedented era of enlightenment has resulted. What mystifies most of us is whether it came about by accident - or through the efforts of an "Invisible Hand."

8
Standing at the Brink

Undoubtedly, the wars, the revolutions and the genocide prevented us from noticing the divine pattern mentioned in the previous chapter. So did the plagues, the famines, the earthquakes and other natural catastrophes. And so did the pain and tears that misery generates. No wonder so many serious thinkers grew cynical. We failed to see the good in the bad, the wisdom in the mistakes - which, one could argue, were aspects of the pattern. And it is understandable why we didn't. No sane person would seek out adversity in order to gain something good. Most persons of good will are repulsed by the thought of something good resulting from the Holocaust or the dropping of an atomic bomb over Hiroshima. For a long time, I could not accept the idea that human suffering could lead to something good. It was true, I thought, that God must be playing games with his creation. I was one of those people who identified with the persecuted, the starving, the homeless, the victims of racism and war, and I was willing to protest on their behalf. But as I grew older, it became clear that good has resulted from natural and man-made disasters. The historical evidence was indisputable.

Chances are the Jews would never have returned to Israel had the Holocaust not happened; and had the A-bomb not been dropped on Japan, the Japanese might have fought to the bitter end, inflicting far more casualties than died in Hiroshima and Nagasaki. The horrors of World War Two created such an impact on humans everywhere that the United

Nations forged an international treaty banning genocide. Most nations have signed it. Consider also: Would the 4 million American slaves been freed as soon as they were had the Civil War not been fought? And because of that war, didn't the young American republic become truly united?

Though colonialism was an instrument of subjugation, in some respects it benefited humankind. Through colonialism, distant cultures were exposed to one another, thus broadening many people's perception of the world. The colonized people - most of them living a tribal existence - were exposed to the concept of nationhood, a necessary step toward globalism. They learned to read and write and develop an appreciation for an education that prepares a person for a profession or vocation and they learned administrative and organizational skills. Though the colonizers had selfish motives and often ruled malevolently, they unwittingly fostered globalism by constructing international communications and transportation networks that linked continents and diverse cultures. As for the colonized, they learned how to improve interpersonal relationships; they discovered new forms of art, music, farming methods and navigation skills. Cultural interaction resulted in intermarriage, which helped to draw the human family closer together.

Because of World War Two, the technology that propelled us into the space age was developed. And more recently, when most of humanity was basking in the glow of hope created by the events in Eastern Europe and Southern Africa, the world was stunned by Iraq's sudden seizure of Kuwait. The reaction was predictable. Many people reverted to their former pessimism, proclaiming with a mixture of sadness and assurance that "as long as humans are around, the world will never enjoy peace." But there was some good that resulted from Iraq's act of aggression: for the first time in history the great majority of nations in the world combined forces to stop an aggressor. They set up an effective international embargo and blockade and organized a powerful military force composed of troops from many nations. A new peace-keeping method had been established, the kind for which Baha'u'llah had called 120 years ago. The world's diplomatic and military response to Iraq was channeled through the United Nations, giving it a powerful boost.

It seems that the concept of paradox is an intrinsic aspect of the flow of life. Scientists and philosophers have identified it as the polarity principle. Certainly Teilhard de Chardin was aware of it. As a young World War One stretcherbearer, he observed: "Through the present war we have really progressed in civilization. To each phase of the world's development there corresponds a certain profoundness of evil ... which integrates with the growing free energy for good."

I know it is repugnant to think that anything good could result from an evil such as war; but in surveying the social evolution of humanity it is apparent that through warfare tribes were forged into nations and feudalism gave way to democracy. After both world wars, the nations of the world attempted to create a new order. The League of Nations was fashioned. Then the United Nations was established with greater powers than its predecessor. With the end of the Cold War we can better appreciate the thesis that all of the wars of the past are leading to the abolition of war as a means of settling disputes. This became evident when the United States and the former Soviet Union signed a series of historic disarmament treaties in the past three years, and started slashing their defense budgets. Their actions caught most of the world by surprise. Both nations finally realized that competing in the arms race was depleting their treasuries, causing critical home-front problems. Besides, the weapons they were producing were far too lethal to use. A nuclear weapons shoot-out would eliminate the human race. So modern warfare, for all intents and purposes, is actually becoming obsolete. It has taken war, and the idea of war, in order for us to appreciate the insanity of war, and agree to eliminate it.

Of course, this new awareness doesn't affect the impulse that drives a person to fight, a condition necessary to wage war. Overcoming that desire requires greater spiritual development - hate must be replaced with love, and prejudice must be replaced with compassion. Cynics would charge that expecting such transformation is unrealistic. But I believe it can be done. It's not easy, considering the moral state of our society. Nevertheless, every human being has been endowed with the capability of supplanting hatred with love. While listening to a lecture and reading a book might help, more is usually required for the transformative process to succeed. It must be demonstrated. Mother Teresa is an example. Interestingly, in demonstrating how she expresses love, patience, kindness and compassion, the polarity principle is operating: without poverty and disease we wouldn't be able to see how she lives and works in the slums of Calcutta - and learn how she maintains such a noble attitude and behavior. Her efforts have inspired others to do what she does.

Though some good can spring from evil, it doesn't mean that evil is a permanent force in life, something absolute, an essence. Evil is actually the absence of good in the same way darkness is the absence of light. Deprive a rose of light and it will wilt. Deprive a human being of divine values, and he'll wilt, so to speak, resorting to lying, cheating, backbiting and violence, if need be, to attain personal goals. When most members of a society aren't practicing divine values they are living in an evil society. What's tragic is that most living in such a setting aren't conscious of becoming willing participants in an evil ideology like Nazism. They are swept up by the prevailing emotions of the day that are generated by a charismatic figure who cleverly exploits the weaknesses, the unfulfilled desires and frustration of his countrymen.

True, at times an evil act can be a necessary glitch and catalyst in the growth pattern of an individual or community. But it seems that life on this plain of existence is a workshop, where we are supposed to strengthen our character, sharpen our intellect and serve our fellow man and community in the spirit of love and unity. To succeed, one needs to internalize and put into practice the divine laws and principles. Before that can be done, however, knowledge of the nature of man is necessary; otherwise application of the laws and principles wouldn't make sense.

There are two aspects to our nature - animal and spiritual. The animal has to do with the body, which is dominated by two essential impulses: survival and reproduction. Without them, the human race would most likely become extinct. Though the body is important, the spirit or soul is more important, for it is the animating force in the human being. From it springs our consciousness. Unlike the body, it is a single entity, not subject to the law of composition and decomposition - it is an eternal essence, whose substance cannot be described, nor its exact connection with the body explained. The only way to explain the relationship is through metaphor: Think of the body as a mirror and the soul as a light trained on the mirror. The light is not within the mirror, nor is it attached to it; for should the mirror fall and break into pieces, the light would continue to shine. When a person neglects to develop his soul, he's dominated by the instincts that drive a beast in the wilderness. Suspicion and fear loom large in his life. Ignorant or defiant of divine laws and principles, he resorts to any means that will get him what he desires. He's usually devoid of conscience, relying on his survival and reproductive drive to succeed in life.

What nourishes the soul? The divine laws and principles that God's messengers reveal from time to time - usually when humanity is groaning for help, appealing for a way to free itself from the dangerous predicaments it continually creates. These extraordinary spiritual figures - a Krishna, Moses, Buddha, Jesus, Mohammed, Baha'u'llah - provide direction on what the purpose of life is; they all remind those whom they come to of God's Grand Design - which, in this day, calls for the unification of the human family. Without that, true world peace cannot be achieved. The Divine Messengers did their job. But the record shows that humanity has faltered in doing its job. Humans are the only creatures in creation with a free will. Unfortunately, we haven't chosen very well. Instead of helping to implement God's Design, man has done the opposite, promoting discord and disunity, often in God's name: the 200-year-old holy war called the Crusades, the Inquisition that tortured and murdered 10 million people; the destruction of the Inca and Aztec civilizations; the participation in black slavery and the condoning of child slavery in Europe are only a few examples.

But despite humanity's blundering, God has intervened in making sure that His design evolves into a dynamic entity. From studying history, as recorded by humans, we can't help but conclude that the divine process is punitive; for there has been so much agony associated with humankind's development. The trail has been steep and tortuous and saturated with blood. Nevertheless, the long, arduous, often reluctant climb has brought us to the point where we find ourselves now, standing bewildered and uncertain at the brink of a phase in our social evolution which the prophets of the past had envisioned. The image of swords being forged into ploughshares is in the process of becoming a reality. God has pushed His stubborn children to its present position - a position pregnant with great promise. Simply put, over the centuries families were pushed into forming clans; clans were pushed into forming tribes; tribes were pushed into forming nations; and now there's movement toward uniting all nations and peoples into one government, with everyone becoming world citizens.

In a way, humanity has had to endure a series of disciplinary actions to get where it is today. The suffering that humanity has had to endure could have been avoided had it faithfully heeded the directions God had given us through His Messengers. It's that simple. Instead, people in the past and present twisted the directions for personal gain; others reduced them to a set of superstitions; while others cast them aside as obsolete notions, becoming ardent worshipers of the finite human mind.

9
The Fate of Tyrants

I know that many people have difficulty accepting the idea that the "Invisible Hand" has always come to the rescue of a confused and desperate humanity, lifting it from the messes it has made. I know that concept always bothered me. But in my search the evidence was clear. In fact, the "Invisible Hand" has always taken notice of those in high office who have openly defied the guidance it has provided humanity. Baha'u'llah issued a warning to those rulers and religious leaders to whom he proclaimed his message: "God hath not blinked nor will He ever blink His eyes at the tyranny of the oppressor. More particularly in this revelation hath He visited each and every tyrant with His vengeance."

Consider what happened to those monarchs and potentates who denounced Baha'u'llah. Napoleon III, who headed the mightiest military machine in the West, was soundly defeated in the Battle of Sedan. Military observers at the time were shocked at the series of battlefield blunders made by him and his brilliant generals. No one could adequately explain the uncharacteristic military actions taken by the French emperor. Not only did he lose his kingdom and was forced to flee France, his only son was killed in the Zulu war, and his beloved country was left in chaos, wracked by a ferocious civil war and years later became a major battlefield in both world wars.

Napoleon's conqueror, William I, Germany's first emperor, also received an epistle from Baha'ullah. In it he warned what would happen to Germany if his counsel wasn't heeded: "O banks of the Rhine! We have seen you covered with gore, inasmuch as the swords of retribution were drawn against you; and you shall have another turn. And we hear the lamentations of Berlin, though she be today in conspicuous glory."

During both world wars humanity witnessed gore blanket the Rhine and heard the lamentations of Berlin. As for the German monarchy - it fell. Two attempts were made on William's life. His successor and eldest son died three months after ascending the throne. William II, who followed, led his nation to defeat in World War I. While he fled to Holland, his country was left economically and politically bankrupt - and ripe for an obscure Austrian paper-hanger, Adolf Hitler, to rise to power. What followed brought unforgettable shame to Germany.

The Austrian Empire disintegrated after its emperor, Francis Joseph, ignored Baha'u'llah's plea. Defeated in World War I, the empire was carved up into several independent nations - and the House of Hapsburgs was dissolved. Austria became a tiny republic that embraced Hitlerism. As for Francis Joseph, he and his family were beset with tragedy and misfortune. His brother Maximillian was killed in Mexico; the crown prince, Randolph, perished in a dishonorable affair; the empress was assassinated in Geneva; Archduke Francis Ferdinand and his wife were murdered in Sarajevo, setting off World War I. Francis Joseph died during the war.

The Russian monarchy suffered a similar fate. Czar Nicolaevich Alexander II was assassinated. His successor, Alexander III, carried out the harsh repressive policies of his predecessor, causing widespread disillusionment and violence in the country, and setting the stage for a revolution that would ultimately lead to the downfall of Imperial Russia. The last czar, Nicolas II and his family, were rounded up by Bolshevik revolutionaries and executed. What filled the political vacuum in Russia was, in many ways, as iron-handed and tyrannical as the rule of the Romanoffs. The Russian Orthodox church was rendered impotent and several million land owners were executed. The 20-year reign of terror orchestrated by dictator Joseph Stalin eliminated much of the nation's intelligentsia and generated a collective fear throughout the land that repressed free expression and movement.

Shortly after receiving an epistle from Baha'u'llah, Pope Pius IX witnessed with deep grief and helplessness the virtual end of the pope's temporal sovereignty. King Victor Emmanuel's forces seized the Papal States - as well as Rome, which had flown the papal flag for 1,000 years. The church's world headquarters was confined to a spit of land in the "Eternal City." All attempts to regain what had been taken proved fruitless. Pope Pius IX 's last years of life were filled with anguish, and he proclaimed himself "a prisoner of the Vatican." Sultan Abdul-'Aziz of the Ottoman Empire, who conspired with his Persian counterpart in banishing and imprisoning Baha'u'llah, was deposed in a palace revolution and four days later assassinated. A nephew who succeeded him was declared an imbecile. After participating on the losing side of World War One, both the empire and sultanate were dissolved and Turkey became a democratic republic.

In Persia, Emperor Nasiri'd-Din Shah, who had the Bab executed and Baha'u'llah imprisoned, and who led a prolonged bloody persecution of the Baha'is, was assassinated. Those who followed him to the Peacock Throne were inept and corrupt rulers. In time, the imperial decay led to the dissolution of the Qajar dynasty. The one that followed also fell in disgrace. What took the place of the two monarchies was a fanatical Shiah Muslim church-state regime that has created a repressive and backward society.

10
Beyond Comprehension

Though we are unable to fathom the workings of the "Invisible Hand", it does what it wishes to do, leaving some of us perplexed, even angry , mainly because of humanity's uncertain condition and the gross injustices and suffering in the world. "Why," many men and women of good will exclaim, "doesn't this mighty force, this universal mind - God - bring about instantaneous global harmony and peace and social justice." "Why," they ask, "are babies dying of starvation?"

While these questions disturb many of us, and keep many of us from accepting the concept of a "loving God, " others who are aware of what cynics see, aware of the world's deprivations, still maintain that God is all-loving. True, trying to figure out how the "Invisible Hand" operates is beyond human comprehension. Attempts to unravel the mystery only lead to hopeless frustration.

However, when we are able to draw away from a crisis, and become emotionally detached , we begin to understand that God doesn't, for example, design and implement famines. The starving masses of Ethiopia and the Sudan, are the result of human selfishness and greed, two negative qualities that spring from our animal side. They are qualities that usually dominate a human being when he hasn't heeded the Divine Educator's exhortations and admonitions on how our Creator expects us to live life.

Enough food and seed were delivered to both countries to avoid starvation. But the life-saving materials were either sold on the black market by greedy government officials, or left to rot in the sand, rather than have the supplies shared with citizens thought to be siding with rebels seeking to overthrow the government. Certainly, the Divine Educators in the past didn't condone that kind of attitude and behavior. Humanity's rejection of their guidance must have been the source of great pain, for they knew what would result from such action. It is the human resistance, avoidance and distorted view of God's guidance that leads society into disrepair, violence, fanaticism and war. It is God's mercy that draws us out of the wreckage we create, and pulls us - often times kicking - closer to the predestined time when the human family will be united, living in peace in a truly unified planet. The "Invisible Hand" is always present.

It doesn't break through a cloud and point the way. Its guidance is given through someone It selects to be a messenger to, and an educator of, humanity. And we are called upon to use our free will to accept the guidance. Some sensitive souls who despair over the world's condition wonder why God doesn't force us to accept His guidance. "It would be so much simpler, and avoid so much pain," they say, "if that were to happen." But God doesn't force us to obey His Messengers, because human beings cease to be human beings when stripped of their power of choice.

Yet, while we are endowed with a free will and use it, God does come to our rescue when the problems we have created are beyond our ability to solve them. The abrupt ending of the Cold War is a case in point. We are faced with choices all the time; some are more complicated and more difficult to make. But none was greater than the one the rulers and ecclesiastical leaders had to make when confronted with Baha'u'llah's challenge. Had they accepted His guidance, world peace would have been established, thus avoiding both world wars and the Cold War - and all of the grief they generated.

Certainly, Baha'u'llah knew that the so called high and mighty would reject His guidance. Yet, his mission called for leading a frightened and narrowly-focused humanity to world unity. First, he assured us that The Kingdom of God on Earth promised by God would be realized - but it would come in two stages. First, the Lesser Peace, followed in time by the Most Great Peace. As we mentioned earlier, the Lesser Peace would come about when the nations of the world begin to unite, each one giving up some of its sovereignty and becoming a state in a world government.

Achieving that condition, he pointed out, wouldn't be easy. Critical choices would have to be made along the way. Serious - and at times tragic - mistakes would be made. Much suffering would be endured, but in the end the Lesser Peace would emerge, taking most men and women by surprise. Surprise - because of people's unawareness of the process that will lead to the inauguration of the Lesser Peace by the end of this century. When will it be fully established? Most likely well into the century. It won't be an accident that will bring it about - nor magic. It is destined to be.

11

Growth and Decline

While humans are destined to be unified and cooperative participants in a global community, the greatest surge toward reaching that glorious day occurred with the coming of the Bab and Baha'u'llah. Prior to their advent there was little apparent movement toward world unity - at least nothing discernible. Not that most people were aware of the movement in the past 100 years. Many people in the past, including some great thinkers, viewed the notion of internationalism as too far fetched, too unrealistic to be realized. They couldn't imagine a world fragmented by national animosities and ethnic and racial prejudices, and plagued by religious strife, coming together. Great minds concocted convincing arguments supporting the thesis that humans were innately incapable of uniting on a local level - let alone, a global level. War and rivalry, they reasoned, were natural characteristics of the human condition, and they cited history to prove their point.

That kind of thinking has prevailed a long time. But when the Cold War ended people began to question some of their fundamental beliefs: T he impossibility of world unity was one of them. The dramatic changes taking place in rapid-fire pace bewildered many people. Skeptics couldn't provide a rational explanation for the gale of change that was sweeping long established traditions and practices into the graveyard of obsolete beliefs.

I wasn't immune to the anxiety the changes produced in people. I needed to know why they occurred. I also needed to know what they would lead to. There were moments when I was afraid to contemplate the future. None of the acknowledged political analysts had acceptable answers. What finally made sense for me was the perspective I found in the Baha'i writings - especially Shoghi Effendi's writings. At first, aspects of what he wrote clashed with my deeply ingrained humanistic views. The idea of divine intervention in human affairs made me uncomfortable. But the more I pondered what Shoghi Effendi shared, the more I realized I had found the right course - the pieces of the puzzle were fitting. It was like finding a lost treasure that many experts doubted existed.

The vision of Shoghi Effendi, the great grandson of Baha'u'llah, helped the most. The late guardian of the Baha'i Faith was the authorized interpreter and expounder of Baha'u'llah's Revelation.

What he shared in the 1930s from his small apartment on Mount Carmel was a brilliant perspective of how the Lesser Peace would materialize. What he wrote was little appreciated by the outside world; and even many Baha'is had difficulty grasping its significance. It seemed too grand a vision, too utopian to be taken seriously. Most people were preoccupied with the popular populists of the day - Hitler, Mussolini and Stalin. These men were dazzling their constituents and others with promises that generated hope in their hearts, pride in their nation and a sense of honor and well-being in a glorious future. And they seemed to be men of their word - they managed to generate fast, dramatic results. Millions of people were drawn to these so-called saviors, and some from different lands. Certainly, the Great Depression was a factor in attracting so many devoted adherents. But it was more than that.

Many who followed Hitler, Mussolini and Stalin saw themselves, for the first time in their lives, as part of a mighty mission that would undo the wrongs of the past while securing a resplendent future. Even the poet Ezra Pound was lured by Mussolini's dream of reviving the Roman Empire. Scientists, churchmen, professors and composers were swayed by Hitler's cry of, "Germany today, and tomorrow the world," and many social idealists around the world viewed the Bolshevik experiment in the Soviet Union as the building of paradise on earth. The exploits of these magnetic leaders were reported daily in the world's press. Radio commentators followed their activities regularly with a sense of awe. In the midst of the commotion over these charismatic ideologues, The League of Nations was collapsing and an unsuspecting humanity was being drawn into the most ferocious and destructive war in history. Unfortunately, not many people heard Shoghi Effendi's call. Or if they did, they didn't grasp its magnitude, its relevance to humanity's destiny. His voice was drowned out by the passionate pronouncements of popular demagogues, and the thunderous cheers of their followers.

Now, 50 years later, as the Baha'i Faith emerges from obscurity and sincere attempts are being made to heal the world's wounds, Shoghi Effendi's vision is beginning to be studied seriously, while the doctrines of Hitler, Mussolini and Stalin are categorized as works of madmen. Establishment of the Lesser Peace won't be marked by a worldwide feeling of euphoria, or a grand international ceremony. It will unfold without most people being aware that it exists. People will be so preoccupied with making the world government work and learning to function in a world society they won't have time to appreciate the historical turn humanity had taken in fulfilling its destiny. Future historians will undoubtedly provide that perspective.

Those of us who are aware of Shoghi Effendi's vision of Baha'u'llah's Revelation have gained some understanding of how the Lesser Peace will materialize. When Baha'u'llah declared that with his coming the old world order would be "rolled up and a new one spread out in its stead, "two processes were launched simultaneously in the world - one of decline, and one of growth. How do they operate? Simply put: What once seemed to work well doesn't anymore; and all attempted adjustments fail, creating anxiety among the faithful. Conversely, new-age ideas are embraced, inspiring some to alter their social, economic and political outlook and understanding of reality - new values evolve.

Each process's pace accelerates, with the passage of time. In other words, the two opposing movements are moving faster and faster in different directions with each passing year, month, even day. As a consequence, more and more established institutions falter; and more and more philosophical and scientific breakthroughs are acknowledged; new ways of doing things are conceived, creating new values that grow more and more appealing to those who are losing faith in the declining old world order. As both processes continually gain momentum, a strange contrast emerges, one that's easily missed in the confusion being generated by the lack of understanding of the swift changes taking place: Every year gets worse than the year before; and every year becomes better than the previous year.

Obviously, evidence of decline is more discernible today than it was in the late 1800s, and will be even more discernible in the near future. Of course, as the dismantling of the old world order becomes more evident, greater fear is engendered. "What will replace the old and tried?" many exclaim. While the growth process accelerates as well, it isn't as apparent to the average person - for his preoccupation with the fear and pain generated by the rolling up of the old world order veils him from noticing the signs of the development of the new world order. Witnessing the dissolution of a familiar way of life, seeing sacred institutions become ineffectual and reliable practices obsolete has been difficult to accept. After all, even if the familiar is flawed, the drive to survive forces humans to make the best of even bad situations.

What seems to frighten people most is replacing what they know with something they haven't experienced. So the immediate reflex is to repress what seems strange or ominous. But there's just so much one can repress. When the number of changes occurring can't be consciously ignored, we become overwhelmed, and confusion sets in - at times, panic. For those who reject the notion of a growth process, yet recognize the decline process, the logical outcome, they believe, has to be human extinction. For the past 50 years this unspeakable thought has plagued more and more people as World War Two raged and the Cold War that followed appeared to be drawing us closer and closer to a nuclear holocaust.

Shoghi Effendi appreciated the reasoning of the doomsayer, for he pointed out that the decline process is leading humanity to barbarism, chaos and ultimate extinction. One doesn't have to build a case to prove that barbarism and chaos are widespread in the world. Watching television news and reading the daily newspaper is evidence enough - not to mention the fear and anxiety and behavioral problems plaguing homes and schools, even churches. Violence and crime are so bad in American cities that parents are outfitting their children with bullet-proof vests. In 1991, more than 24,000 murders were reported in the United States.

Shoghi Effendi didn't forecast the obliteration of the human race, for he was very much aware of the growth process and where that was headed. As the decline process gains more and more momentum, more men and women would grow disenchanted with the ways and operations of the established order and embrace new-age values and affiliate with new-age organizations - all products of the growth process. When a critical mass of people involved in new-age thinking and action is formed, the foundation of the Lesser Peace will be in place. They will be ready to take the two steps, Shoghi Effendi pointed out, that have to be taken before the Lesser Peace is fully established: first, the political unification of the Eastern and Western Hemispheres; and, second, the establishment of a world government.

12
Conservatives vs. Liberals

While both processes operate in the world, they are interdependent. Without decline, there would be no need for growth - there would be no need for change. Traditionally, humans accept new ideas and practices when the old ones are failing. Generally, political participants view change from one of two perspectives: conservatives and liberals. Both are involved in the decline process and, through their actions, unwittingly contribute to its acceleration.

The conservatives, who view new ideas as a threat to their security, cling tenaciously to laws, principles and traditions that are supposed to preserve the status quo. To solve problems, they try to draw from lessons learned in the past; they apply antiquated laws to deal with modern issues. This is true in the political, economic, social and religious arenas. Firm in their convictions, they tend to resist new ideas. The more resistance they encounter, the more rigid they become. How they oppose new ideas is a matter of degree. Extremist groups like the Ku Klux Klan or the neo Nazis are willing to resort to any means - including violence - to defend what they believe is right and promote their cause. Moderate conservatives won't resort to violence, taking instead the political and propaganda routes. In curbing crime, for example, the extremists will defy existing law and organize vigilante squads, whereas the moderates will advocate legislation that will give the police greater power and make it easier for civilians to purchase guns.

Both factions give little credence to the liberal approach of trying to unearth the causes of crime and eliminate them through educational schemes and decent jobs. Usually, employing the conservatives' so-called Law and Order approach backfires, creating more tension than existed before. As a result the process of decline is fueled. When the police get tougher so do the criminals, who gain more recruits from the socially and economically underdeveloped communities that have always been a potential breeding ground for outlaws. Crime and violence increases, heightening the fear, anger and hopelessness in the community. School interest among children and youth falters - many drop out without employable skills. A growing group of restless, unemployed individuals emerges, seeking something that will improve their economic and social standing in the community. When legal employment isn't available, they gravitate toward illegal forms of work - like drug peddling - which further stimulates the decline process's pace.

But it's not only the poor who are enmeshed in the process of decline. The rich and middle class are involved as well. The suicide rate among suburbanites of all ages is on the rise. Drug and alcohol abuse among the financially secure is rising. So are broken homes and white collar crimes. The continual erosion of what was once considered wholesome infuriates and frightens conservatives. Many dig in their heels and grow more rigid in resisting change. They become obsessed with preventing any liberal cause from influencing their community. What usually escapes them is the fact that what they're defending resulted from a liberal cause. Those who engineered the American Revolution were radical leftists, the kind of people who the modern day, super-patriotic American rightists would have difficulty accepting. Ten years after the radical Bolshevik Revolution, the Soviet Union's leadership grew conservative, crushing all internal attempts to reform established procedures.

No matter how hard conservatives try to shore up obsolete laws and practices, they are unable to stop the rampaging decline of the only way of life they know. Frightened, they try to withdraw from the promiscuity and alienation caused, they believe, by liberal movements. But it is difficult to escape from what they feel is decadent. They're surrounded by forces they abhor, forces that have infiltrated radio, television, the cinema, magazines, the schools, the churches, even topics of conversation. Their anger, bitterness and suspicion grows daily, fueling their antagonism toward everything liberal, which, in turn, fuels the already highly-charged negative atmosphere in a rapidly declining society.

The liberals are contributing to the decline process as well, despite wholehearted efforts to reverse the seemingly irreversible slide. Like the conservatives, most of them want to preserve their society. Where they differ is in philosophy and method. Both want peace, for example, but maintain a different focus in obtaining their goal. Liberals push disarmament, while conservatives clamor for a stronger military force as the only means of preventing war.

The conservative-liberal feud festers in economic, social and religious realms. There are liberal and conservative wings in the Democratic and Republican Parties, within the Roman Catholic hierarchy, in Judaism, in the judiciary, in high finance, among the Communists, and even the family. The friction and bickering caused by the feuds have helped to quicken the rolling up of the old world order. There are many shades of liberalism. The extremists, who are few in number, won't hesitate to employ violence to gain an objective. In the Sixties, the Students for Democratic Action and the Yippies gained notoriety by bombing research plants where sophisticated weaponry was being designed. There are still pockets of active liberal extremists like the Red Brigades in Italy, Germany, Japan and South Korea. From time to time they strike out violently against what they believe to be reactionary elements in society. Other extremists act out their hostility toward conventional thinking and behavior by flaunting their hedonism in public, wearing outrageous fashions and hairdos. Most liberals, however, wear suits and dresses and advocate causes like abortion, disarmament, ecological clean-up, women's rights, social justice for the poor and persecuted, and peace. They lobby for new laws, try to educate the public about their causes, and develop new practices - all designed to reform the existing system. In a crunch, they'll organize and march on a picket line.

What plagues the liberal movement is a lack of unity. There are thousands of liberal groups with their own agendas, creating new concepts, new social and economic schemes, demanding new laws. Their competition for the minds of men and women in the pro-peace camp, for example, has set off intra-camp feuding. What's lacking is an authority that can consolidate their ideas and goals - and unify them into a cohesive force. Without that, they unwittingly sow the seeds of anarchy. And because conservatives believe that's happening, their resolve to resist everything liberal intensifies - and the process of decline accelerates. They blame the liberals for the break down of morality and the growing scourge of drug and alcohol addiction in society. And the liberals counter by citing conservatives' repressive and obsolete social and religious practices and laws as the cause of people's drift to drugs and alcohol and immorality.

Of course, there are those who support aspects of both conservative and liberal causes. While opposing abortion, for instance, they may promote racial unity. Hard core conservatives and liberals consider those who split their affiliation as traitors. While most people fall in the so-called "traitor" category, they lack the zeal and fervor that the ideologues possess. Moderates tend to exhibit moderate behavior, allowing themselves to be carried along by the flow of events. They are watching, waiting, trying to determine where to turn to when the situation grows completely out of hand.

While the feuding intensifies, the delineation between liberal and conservative is blurred. What starts as a liberal enterprise evolves into a conservative cause, and vice versa. What doesn't change is the battling. What has led to the depletion of Brazil's rain forests is a classical example of how conservative-liberal feuding fuels the process of decline. All sorts of damage has been done - and not only to the environment. In a liberal gesture, the Brazilian government has granted free Amazon region acreage to anyone willing to farm it for at least five years. A financial subsidy has been offered as well. To Brazil's poor - especially the sharecroppers - it is a dream come true. The idea of becoming a landowner, of becoming economically independent for the first time in their lives has drawn thousands of men, women and children to the Amazon adventure. With meager belongings, families have streamed to what has always been considered forbidden territory. Unsubstantiated stories of Indian atrocities against Eastern homesteaders and of man-eating jaguars haven't deterred the pioneers.

The government has been cheered by the response, because development of the virginal rainforest expanse would bolster the nation's economy. Rich mineral resources exist in the region. Development also means physically linking the undeveloped west with the developed east. Not only have the poor taken advantage of the government's offer. Rich entrepreneurs, with government connections, have secured the largest

74

tracts of land - in some cases 10,000 to 20,000 acres. Towns have suddenly sprung up to service the settlers' agricultural and domestic needs. Saloons and whorehouses have followed. The discovery of gold has lured thousands more who are feverishly clawing hillsides for the precious metal. Chain-saw wielding lumbermen have also arrived, as have numerous construction crews with their thundering bulldozers.

Environmentalists in Brazil and elsewhere have pleaded for an end to the rape of the Amazon rain forest - nature's greatest manufacturer of oxygen. The settlers have ignored the plea. So has the government. Economic progress, they have felt, is more important than scientists' high-minded views proclaimed from comfortable university laboratories.

The lust for quick riches has resulted in a breakdown of morality and law and order. Local officials have been corrupted by the wealthy landowners, many of whom are getting hefty subsidies from the government. The more land a settler develops, the greater subsidy he gets. Some are getting a million dollars a year; and it doesn't matter that the land hasn't been farmed and the owners have been living in their Rio de Janeiro and Sao Paulo estates. Heavily armed private security guards have been protecting the absentee landlords' property.

For most of the settlers, the farming venture has failed. The soil is too poor to yield profitable crops. But the former sharecroppers have remained in the region, some returning to sharecropping, while others have become squatters on the wealthy landowners' ranches, where the soil is believed to be more productive.

Bloody conflicts have ensued between squatters and ranch security guards. At least 1,000 people have been killed. The casualties are expected to mount, for the struggle hasn't been resolved. Nor has the plight of the Indians, who have been pushed deeper into the rain forest. Alarmed at what the settlers have been doing to their homeland and their way of life, the Indians have fought back - often, raiding settlements, and killing or abducting the "intruders." Such provocations have triggered retaliation by settler vigilante groups and the government police.

The Indians have suffered in other ways. Exposure to settlers' diseases has proven to be deadly. Some resistance to taking the "intruders'" medicine has compounded the problem. Not only is the Indian population dwindling, but thousands of plant and animal species in the rain forest - vital to medical drug development - have been wiped out by

75

the incessant land clearing operations. In the Amazon development project, we have witnessed considerable evidence of the barbarism, chaos and ultimate extinction that Shoghi Effendi said would result as the process of decline quickens.

13

In the New World

While the growth process isn't as evident as its counterpart, decline, it is very much alive. Because of the dramatic events in Eastern Europe, Southern Africa, and the Middle East, more individuals and some institutions are beginning to notice it. In fact, diplomats and journalists have added a new phrase to their vocabulary - "The emerging new world order." Interestingly, they mouth the term with little understanding of what shape the new world order will take, and how it will impact on humanity. Yet, they speak of it as something inevitable. Yes, the same people who only a few months earlier rejected the notion of a global society have embraced the idea! What has caused the change of focus?

"The Invisible Hand." Now, it wasn't an unprecedented shove. The "Invisible Hand" has been guiding humanity all along - through the stages of infancy, childhood, adolescence, and is presently guiding us through a twilight period, somewhere between adolescence and maturity. As the growth process accelerates with each passing day, we're drawn closer to adulthood. Understanding of our condition grows. We are becoming aware of our adolescent stage and the deviant behavior associated with it. The thought of reverting to it repels us. By gaining a glimpse of the next stage, we are impelled to reach it; we want to reach it so badly we are beginning to exercise our will to secure what seems irresistible.

During our childhood phase, the great mass of humanity was dependent on powerful authoritarian figures or institutions for survival and development. Prior to the 19th century most people sought protection and guidance from kings, feudal lords and the priesthood - just as a present-day 5-year-old seeks security from his parents.

In the mid-1800s, humanity exhibited its first signs of adolescence. People began to assert themselves, seeking independence from age-old institutions and traditions. Despite erratic and at times irrational behavior, their exploits gained popularity, causing change, chaos and confusion. As the growth process accelerated with the passage of time, the chaos and confusion intensified, as did the pain. As parents can attest, those children struggling with adolescence are preoccupied with power, pleasure and love; are obsessed with personal gain, suffering from swings between immaturity and flashes of maturity. So it has been with the human race.

Self-centered nations consumed with suspicion clashed over petty issues. Greed powered the business community. As psychiatrist Hussein Danesh points out, we were afflicted by a "good guy" versus "bad guy" mentality. Narcissism abounded. Most of us have lived through it, have participated in it. We have functioned with an adolescent mentality, viewing the world from an unhealthy adolescent perspective. Consequently, our art, music, clothes, food, work habits, personal ambitions, sexual orientation and value systems have been, for the most part, those of an adolescent. Immersed in adolescence, humanity has exhibited a lack of emotional balance; a lack of objectivity. Yet we have made progress, stumbling ever closer to maturity - the "Invisible Hand" always available to prevent us from slipping off the edge.

What are the signs that signify that humanity has reached the threshold of maturity? The developing collective realization that something must be done to eradicate racism, elevate the status of women with men, eliminate hunger and disease, provide education for all, and put an end to the carnage being committed to the Earth's ecology. Along with this realization is a growing awareness that in order to achieve what has to be done is a need for universal cooperation - all peoples working through an international agency that has the authority to carry out what is deemed best for the global community.

In August of 1990 we witnessed that kind of cooperation when the United Nations - with the strong support of most governments - took swift and definitive action against Iraq for seizing Kuwait. A shipping and air blockade was installed against the Baghdad regime. Seeing former Cold

War enemies working hand-in-hand through the leadership of the United Nations was not only an encouraging sign to people everywhere - it was a sign that, finally, humanity was reaching the stage of maturity. No single nation acted impulsively. Decisions were made through consultation at the U.N. Security Council. The participants exhibited patience, compassion and wisdom - all attributes of the mature.

Because the American news media was so "old world order-focused," it missed the big story at the Helsinki Summit. Had the United States and the Soviet Union agreed to a joint military assault on Iraq (an adolescent act), the journalists would have felt that something newsworthy resulted from the Summit. Instead, they down-played the Bush-Gorbachev decision to funnel all authority to the United Nations in handling the Iraqi issue - an unprecedented collective security act that set an example of how to deal with future geopolitical aberrations in the world. The United States and the Soviet Union - the world's greatest military powers at the time - didn't act impetuously. While acting in a mature fashion, exhibiting patience and avoiding immediate unilateral military action, they didn't shrink from their responsibility to find a just solution to the crisis.

Through consultation they decided to support wholeheartedly the United Nations' efforts, stressing sanctions and blockade as the first steps to a solution. But more important - in the spirit of cooperation, they displayed a genuine willingness to follow the lead of the United Nations, abandoning the adolescent qualities of arrogance and cockiness that both countries often exhibited in confronting critical international conflicts in the past. Of course, there were some anxious moments, when the United States seemed to be losing patience, showing signs of wanting to attack Iraq alone. Old habits are hard to break! In the past the United States would have taken unilateral action, or tried to persuade its allies to join in a military venture. Though military action had to be resorted to, it was the result of U.N. Security Council consultation.

It's important to keep in mind that the promising position the world finds itself today didn't come about suddenly. It only seemed sudden, because most of us weren't aware of the growth process functioning even during both world wars and the Cold War. During those horrible periods our global consciousness began to develop. We became acquainted with unfamiliar peoples and lands. With the advent of nuclear weapons we became aware of how small and vulnerable our planet is, and many realized for the first time that all humans share a common home - Earth. Small groups of inspired souls unwittingly plugged into the creative energy unleashed with the coming of Baha'u'llah, promoting causes he advocated in the mid-1800s. Human rights, women's rights, economic justice, child advocacy, disarmament, ecological protection, free trade, universal literacy, global medical and world federalism movements emerged, all chipping away at the barriers developed during humanity's childhood and adolescence. Though not formally connected, their activity is helping to influence people, of all strata of society, to consider new options to "old world order" ways of doing things, ways that are incapable of solving the planet's pressing contemporary problems.

Advanced communications technology aids the chipping away effort. There has been a steady proliferation of new world order ideas appearing on billboards, ads, TV, radio, books, newspapers and magazines seeping into people's consciousness, preparing the way for the Lesser Peace. Through the communications satellite, new world order ideas and projects are shared with people everywhere through broadcasting and cable television, radio and the print media. People's consciousness is being raised; their vision is being broadened. They notice aspects of reality they never noticed before. Better informed, they are demanding changes. United Nations agencies like the UN Children's Fund, UN Educational, Scientific and Cultural Organization, the World Health Organization, the UN Conference on Trade and Development, the Food and Agricultural Organization, the International Bank for Reconstruction and Development, the World Meteorological Organization and many other groups are publishing and distributing literature and holding conferences and workshops throughout the world, promoting new world order ideas. Grassroots movements are doing the same thing. Greenpeace, for example, has set up chapters on all continents, publishes an international magazine, has organized an active speakers' bureau, and has recruited professors and scientists to become involved in its mission to persuade humanity to stop polluting the planet. After several years of work, the World Constitution and Parliament Association forged "A Constitution for the Federation of Earth." At a Constituent Assembly in 1977, participants from 25 countries, from every continent, signed the document, which includes steps toward establishing a world government. News of its existence is spreading. Over 5 million people have endorsed it. Amnesty International combs the planet for human rights violations. By sharing its findings, violators are shamed into stopping their persecution and torture of minorities. This grassroots human rights monitoring agency coordinates its activities with various U.N. agencies. As a consequence, despots can no longer hide their human rights crimes from the world.

The highly-respected Club of Rome, a futurist think tank that studies global trends, finds that humanity is developing a world consciousness. To accommodate that phenomenon, it recommends the establishment of a world government. The Club of Rome's findings are shared with other think tanks, universities around the world and the news media, which share them with the general public.

The 1,500 peace groups, located in some 50 nations, are disseminating information that is helping to crack antiquated beliefs that most people harbor. They are providing compelling reasons why change is needed in humanity's priorities - reasons like: " ... Seven month's worth of world military spending would be enough to pay for supplying clean water supplies and adequate sanitation for as many as two billion people ... who now lack these bare essentials of life," or, "Fifty million children's lives can be saved annually if the money spent in 20 hours for armaments was available to feed and heal the world's neglected youngsters."

More and more information like that is reaching more and more people, which is contributing to the abandonment of old world order thinking and behavior, leaving many looking for something more meaningful to believe in. Some are finding what they yearn for by leaving the decline process flow for the constantly accelerating growth process - which is leading humankind to the fulfillment of its glorious destiny.

Prominent social observers have noticed the movement towards globalism - people like Robert Muller, the former assistant secretary general of the United Nations: "There was a pattern in all this. Something gigantic was going on, a real turning point in evolution," he wrote in "New Genesis," "the beginning of an entirely new era of which international cooperation at the United Nations was only a first outward reflection."

14

Behind the Power

As humanity emerges from the labyrinth of adolescence and is drawn to the light of maturity, it becomes more spiritually conscious, shedding its suspicion, hostility , anger, arrogance, and selfishness and starts growing more trusting, more compassionate, more caring, more patient - viewing humility as a strength, not a weakness.

The late visionary and scientist, Teilhard de Chardin, noticed the quickening spirit of transformation in the world: "Everywhere on Earth, at this moment, in the new spiritual atmosphere created by the idea of evolution, there floats, in a state of extreme mutual sensitivity, love of God and faith in the world, the two essential components of the Ultrahuman. These two components are everywhere 'in the air'... sooner or later there will be a chain reaction. "Could this remarkable process of change we are witnessing be the result of a series of accidents? Believing that is like believing that a set of encyclopedias can be produced through an explosion in a printing press. The "Invisible Hand" is behind what Chardin saw happening.

Some of the highly learned among us who recognize this transformation taking place can appreciate the guidance given by God. While they acknowledge the guidance, they are aware of their powerlessness to fathom the essence of its Provider, or comprehend the way in which the guidance is given. They are secure in knowing that no amount of scientific probing will provide an accurate accounting of the essence that is God.

That belief is continually reinforced as they continue to explore the origin and operation of creation. The more they probe, the more impressed they become of the magnificent complexity, the wonder of all life.

Scientist Max Planck can attest to that: "As a physicist, and therefore as a man who has spent his whole life in the service of the driest science, the investigation of matter, I am surely free from the suspicion of being a fanatic; and so, after my investigation of the atom, I tell you this: There is not matter in and of itself. All matter originates and subsists only through a power which brings the atomic particles into oscillation and holds them together in the tiniest solar system, which is the atom ... Thus, behind this power we must assume that there is a knowing, intelligent spirit. This spirit is the ground of all matter. It is not the visible but transient matter which is real, genuine, true; rather the invisible, immortal spirit is the reality. I do not hesitate to name this mysterious Creator as all the ancient people of the earth in earlier centuries named Him: God."

Though the essence of God is unfathomable, God's presence is everywhere, acting not as a neutral spectator but as a loving parent. Though to the limited human eye the suffering and confusion we witness in the world may give us the impression that life is a continuous "crap-shoot," there is a reason for everything that occurs. The fact that we can't understand this fundamental universal law doesn't invalidate it. In some respects, rejecting that law is like rejecting the fact that our planet is constantly spinning and is on a continuous journey around our sun. While we can't see the spinning or sense Earth's ongoing celestial trip, it doesn't negate the fact that that's what's actually happening.

God is involved in humanity's struggle to reach maturity. Operating in the world today, according to Shoghi Effendi, are two Divine Plans - a major one and a minor one. The processes of decline and growth stem from God's Major Plan, propelling us - at times precariously - to the Lesser Peace. No one is able to identify its functional pattern. Whatever we know about it is based on what has resulted from it. It is unpredictable, appears disorderly - and moves mysteriously. Perhaps the best description of how God's Major Plan is being implemented has been made by The Universal House of Justice, the Baha'i Faith's international ruling body: "The Major Plan is tumultuous in its progress, working through mankind as a whole, tearing down barriers to world unity, forging mankind into a unified body in the fires of suffering and experience."

Though not a Baha'i, scientist Ervin Laszlo senses the fundamental truth of the Universal House of Justice's observation: "The general direction of historical evolution is not different from the general direction of evolution in nature. It climbs toward the highest-level system through sudden bursts of creativity that come in the wake of critical instabilities. "The truly hopeful signs of our times are not the struggles of the present international system to achieve some form of worldwide status quo, for whatever progress is achieved is far too slow and far too inadequate to stem the tide of growing crises. Rather, the hopeful signs are the crises themselves: the progressive destabilization of today's obsolete world system, with its national interests, national jealousies, narrow competitiveness and blindness to the most elementary imperatives of human survival. For it is out of this chaos that the new order will come, it is out of the ashes of the present international disorder that the phoenix of the world order prophesied in the Baha'i writings will arise."

Fortunately, while God's Major Plan unfolds, God's Minor Plan is unfolding as well. In reality, they are interrelated. Without the Minor Plan humanity would find itself in a terrible predicament - ready to go to a highly prized destination, but not knowing how to reach it, and not knowing what to do once there. Part of Baha'u'llah's mission was to reveal God's Minor Plan - and launch it. Unlike the Major Plan, its moves and results are predictable. Because its directions are clear, it is implemented in an orderly fashion. The writings of Baha'u'llah, Abdul Baha and Shoghi Effendi are explicit as to what has to be done to carry out God's Minor Plan. They function as a blueprint for peace at a time when the great masses of humanity grope desperately for that kind of guidance. Baha'u'llah's growing number of followers have the responsibility of implementing it. As Baha'is implement the Plan, humanity will gain the guidance and inspiration needed to create a world civilization that will evolve into the Kingdom of God on Earth. For what the Baha'is are busy building is meant to function as a model - their gift to the rest of the human family.

By carrying out the Divine Blueprint, Baha'is internalize and put into practice human development principles that prepare them to fulfill their spiritual obligation, which is to help unify humankind and spiritualize the planet. They are busy building communities where the love of God drives them to overcome their prejudices, recognize the reality of the oneness of humankind, work for the equality of the sexes, develop a giving spirit and a prayerful attitude, perfect the ability to consult in a mature fashion, make community service an integral part of their lives, view work as a form of worship, and find joy in helping others.

Since the mid-1800s, Baha'is on all five continents have developed a network of communities based on principles that people in the future will live by in a world society. So in a sense, Baha'is are living in the future as well as the present, paving the way for populations yet unborn.

God hasn't forsaken us. While tearing down the old world order - with all of its dehumanizing imperfections - He has provided the means to create a model for living in a world civilization that will be responsible for constructing His Kingdom on Earth. The model which is presently being perfected represents what a harassed humanity, in an emerging new world order, is desperately searching for. Sadly, most people aren't aware of it, even though it probably exists in their town.

Many religious people, especially Christians, are expecting the Kingdom of God to come about dramatically - in an instant. They await a heavenly miracle. Many others have abandoned that belief and either grope blindly for something meaningful to believe in, or have given up hope of ever finding something to believe in, resigning themselves to a dog-eat-dog kind of existence. Then there are those who are caught up in the flow of the growth process - sensing that something good is about to happen. They don't know what exactly it is going to be. All they know is that, in the long run, it is going to benefit them and everyone else. The longer they remain in the growth flow the more optimistic they become, and the more aware they grow of God's influence in the development of humanity's destiny.

As the number of Baha'i communities expand - all trying to internalize God's principles for living in a new world order - many of those caught up in the growth process flow will notice the Minor Plan in operation. While they won't identify it as such, they'll nevertheless be attracted to it by what it is doing in transforming individuals and groups. While in the midst of those trying to perfect the model, they'll find themselves immersed in an environment they always longed to experience but had given up hope of ever finding. In that atmosphere, they will gain some understanding of what the new world order will most likely be like. For they will be exposed to a trusting people of all skin colors, of all socio and economic strata creating a community based on love and unity. Moved, they will want to become full-time participants in what they are experiencing - and commit themselves to sharing with others a way of life preordained by God - an experience that represents the last remaining refuge of a tottering civilization.

As this phenomenon occurs more and more, the ranks of those implementing God's Minor Plan will evolve into a critical mass. At that time, humanity will begin to appreciate the fact that the Kingdom of God on Earth has been in the process of being constructed - albeit, painstakingly - while nations have been pummeling each other during two world wars and terrorizing each other during the Cold War. It hasn't been winged humanoids with halos hovering over their heads that have been doing the building. For the most part, ordinary folks have been doing the work - trying to follow the principles laid down in God's Minor Plan. Not only within the Baha'i community, but at work and at play - everywhere. For the first 140 years their labors attracted little or no attention. Most social observers who peeked into the Baha'i community came away with the notion that its adherents were a group of gentle and kindly men and women with lofty ideas that weren't relevant to modern day needs.

Working in virtual obscurity, the Baha'is have forged ahead, quietly and resolutely, laying the foundation of a new world order. It hasn't been glamorous work. In fact, it has been downright difficult and painful at times. Overcoming one's prejudices hasn't been easy; learning to love someone you feel is unlovable can be an agonizing test; and building a united community composed of professors, illiterates, bankers, grave diggers, blacks, whites, Asians, Latinos and American Indians, introverts and extroverts, old and young, rich and poor, counter culture people and corporate executives - has been a spiritual responsibility they have had to tackle - if they were to remain faithful. For the most part, they have been doing it, knowing full well that continual effort is necessary in order to maintain unity. Their communities have been social laboratories, producing people prepared to live and work in a new world order. What sustains their interest in what they are doing is the perspective they receive from their sacred text. It fuels the fire of their enthusiasm; it fortifies their resolve to press onward when seemingly insurmountable obstacles arise.

For example, Baha'is the world over - in Ecuador, Iceland, Kenya, Micronesia, India and in every other land - are exposed to holy writings that puts their mission in sharp focus: "Verily, God has chosen you for His love and knowledge; God has chosen you for the worthy service of unifying mankind; God has chosen you for the purpose of investigating reality and promulgating international peace; God has chosen you for the progress and development of humanity, for spreading and proclaiming true education, for the expression of love toward your fellow creatures and the removal of prejudice; God has chosen you to blend together human hearts and give light to the human world. The doors of His generosity are wide, wide open to us; but we must be attentive, alert and mindful, occupied with service to all mankind, appreciating the bestowals of God and ever conforming to His will."

The press has taken little note of what the Baha'is are doing. Occasionally, a local newspaper reports on a race unity meeting that attracts 50 people or more. Sometimes, a noted speaker at a Baha'i conference leads to some news media coverage. The only time the world press does a story on the Baha'is is when they are being persecuted. Journalists aren't covering the Baha'i effort to build the framework for a new world order, because they think the well-meaning small band of spiritual minded men and women are engaged in a futile exercise.

Criticized for their refusal to participate in partisan politics, Baha'is developed a reputation, in some social activist circles, as hopeless idealists. Other old-world-order focused activist groups have viewed the Baha'is' stand on politics as foolish. Without political power, they claim, meaningful societal changes won't occur. It isn't that the Baha'i Faith is opposed to politics as a means of getting things done. It's simply engaged in a different form of politics, the politics of unity. It rejects the present-day political systems, because they are too narrowly focused, established to run obsolete nationalistic oriented institutions, not a global society.

If Baha'is were involved in the present-day political schemes, the model of community unity they have been building over the years would not exist. They would be members of different political parties, expending most of their energy beating out the opposition. In essence they would be busy perpetuating disunity, not unity. More and more people are recognizing what Baha'is have felt for decades. Low turnouts in U.S. elections, even presidential elections, is a sign of a lack of faith in the existing political processes. The growing urge to oust incumbent legislators is another sign. In the United States, a 1990 CNN and Time Magazine poll reported that 89 percent of those polled disapproved of the way Congress was functioning. People in a number of states have voted to limit the time legislators can serve in the legislature. Even lawmakers are deeply concerned. Senator Warren Rudman, a highly respected independent-minded lawmaker, deplores what is happening: "The daily drumbeat of scandals, all given star billing with no distinction as to seriousness, is reverberating throughout society. It is leading to cynicism, apathy and perhaps a general attitude that lawlessness is in some way condoned or overlooked among the elite and powerful. This in turn becomes an excuse to justify one's own misbehavior, and soon respect for the law is lost."

Communism, once hailed by many idealists as the political panacea, has failed. Those who lived in Marxist societies grope for new direction. Exposure of more and more corrupt politicians in democracies has shaken citizens' faith in their government. The deterioration of their nation's social and economic infrastructure is being blamed on the politicians. People yearn for a form of governance run by men and women who are guided by moral principles, who view their responsibilities as an opportunity to improve the social and economic health of their community. There appears to be a universal longing for change, for an infusion of fresh spiritual energy. People are fed up with the prevailing order. But most are caught in a dilemma. While they yearn for change, they're afraid of it; for what replaces the existing system could be worse than what they presently have. They don't know where to turn for help. Demagogues abound, promoting quick-fix schemes. People who have been fooled once fear being fooled again. For they know there is no greater pain than discovering what you have wholeheartedly embraced is a fraud.

Within Baha'i communities around the world, men and women are perfecting a divinely revealed political system, in which no individual has authority. There are no political parties; no election campaigns; no special slate of candidates; no caucusing; no party platforms; no vested interest lobbying; no political party machines; no political bosses. Because it is based on spiritual principles, its view of power is different than the prevailing view. Social and economic status holds no special influence in the Baha'i community. Though academic and cultural attainment is admired and respected, such accomplishments aren't used to build a political power base. In fact, Baha'is have been conditioned to spot any sign of political ambition in their community. When they do, it is a signal not to vote for a person who exhibits such a trait. Baha'i power is not based on gaining dominance and control; it is based on service.

When Abdul Baha was asked by a Cleveland news reporter in 1912 to sum up his faith in one sentence, he said, "My religion is perpetual service to the human race. "To a Baha'i, a powerful person is humble, modest, selfless, genuine, truthful, generous, truly happy, someone who prefers others over himself, and is actively engaged in the process of knowing and loving God, acquiring virtues and being involved in helping to make the world a better place by making his community a better place. In time, he believes, these communities will come together.

In the Baha'i Faith, authority is vested in local, national and international elected bodies - which have executive, legislative, judicial and unific responsibilities. Elections to these bodies are executed via secret ballot. The voter considers spiritual development an important factor in those he votes for. Those who serve on these bodies are not privileged people who respond to the electorate's needs only in time of crisis. Their response to calls for help from community members are motivated by altruism, not a desire to gain support for re-election. Decisions made by these governing bodies are arrived at through consultation. The vast body of Baha'i writings is used as a guide to the consultative process. Every member's contribution is sought and appreciated. When a thought is expressed or an idea shared, it is offered as a gift to the community. While pushing one's ideas is frowned upon, providing as much information as possible to support an idea is encouraged. A safeguard against the former happening is purity of motive and humility. And those qualities are acquired by making a sincere effort to grow spiritually.

Those serving on a governing body are conditioned to sense when a fellow member strays from the course. Baha'i decision-making is like a collective sculpting exercise. Someone offers an idea. If it seems to have merit, other suggestions are made to improve the original idea. Often, all nine members of the governing body are involved in molding the idea into a decision. Usually, the end result is different than what was originally suggested. When that happens, the originator of the idea is not offended; for his purpose in giving it is to help the community, not to promote himself.

Total community involvement in administrating its affairs is encouraged. For example, every 19 days the entire community assembles to pray together, break bread together and consult on important issues. This gathering is actually a Baha'i institution, where everyone, including children, is encouraged to make recommendations to the local governing body. Because the local governing body views itself as a servant of the community, it takes all recommendations to heart. What is done with a recommendation is based on its relevance to the community's needs. At the next gathering, decisions on all recommendations are revealed. It is important to note that every recommendation that is made springs from a sincere desire to help. On the other hand, its recipient appreciates the recommendations and urges the community to continue to make them. The interaction sharpens the way the community is administered, for the governing body is continually receiving fresh ideas. This process also fosters community oneness, for those not serving on the local governing body know they have a say in the way their community is administered - and that their opinion is valued. With that understanding, a member of the Baha'i community tends to live his faith throughout the week. Not dependent on clergy assistance, he's a full-time participant in the process of helping his community become a healthier spiritual and social entity.

Working on a governing body isn't viewed as a job, but rather an ongoing act of service - and love. Though a non-paying responsibility, it is usually carried out with a dedication fueled by a deep love of God and an awareness of a believer's duty to participate in implementing God's Minor Plan. Seeking membership on the governing body is frowned upon. However, when elected one serves conscientiously. The positive attitude stems from an allegiance to an authority, which a Baha'i considers a caring parent who knows what's best for him. The opportunity to serve on a governing body has its personal rewards. Being involved in the process of administrating to the affairs of the community, you usually grow spiritually; for you're exposed to more and more of Baha'u'llah's laws and standards. It is these laws and standards that determine the decisions that a Baha'i governing body makes.

At this juncture in the development of the Baha'i Administrative Order, all of its 18,000 local governing bodies are in varying degrees of maturity. Making the transition from old world order ways of doing things to the new world order way hasn't been easy. Aspects of one's culture sometimes become stumbling-blocks. For many, the transformation process has been painful. Mistakes are made, especially when old world order ways are unwittingly employed in Baha'i projects. Many of the mistakes made are due to years of old world order conditioning. Those who serve on a Baha'i governing body are not beholden to any constituency. They are to focus on serving and improving the commonweal, using the Baha'i teachings as a guide.

In time - as Baha'is grow closer to the teachings of their faith, internalizing them and practicing them with conviction, their community becomes a spiritual magnet within the community-at-large. This is already happening, especially in Latin America, Africa, South East Asia, the Pacific Islands and India. For example, in some countries people who aren't Baha'is go to the local Baha'i governing body to settle disputes and seek justice. A governor of an Indian state asked the Baha'is to draft a curriculum for moral education - to be taught only by Baha'is in every public school.

In villages made up primarily of Baha'is, schools are built, medical clinics are established, and the equality of the sexes is promoted. In one region of Zaire recently, a women's conference was held, where the men volunteered to mind the children and cook the meals. Government officials were astonished at the dramatic change in attitude of those men who had become Baha'is.

As the dismantling of the old world order in Europe and North America accelerates, some people there are beginning to notice the Baha'i community and are being drawn to it, seeking perspective and meaning to the puzzling, dramatic changes that are taking place. Realizing that the old world order of doing things is obsolete, they seek new direction, they seek communities where hope and optimism are apparent just by the way its members look and speak; they seek a community where people genuinely care for one another regardless of their surname, skin color or ethnic background. They yearn to live in a place free of corruption, deceit, a place where cooperation and unity are practiced wholeheartedly. For the most part, they find all of that in the local Baha'i community. They're also intrigued by the Baha'i outlook on life, and its refreshing view of reality. Exposed to new world order views, they recognize that they, like most other people, have accepted distorted aspects of reality as reality.

Most people today are steeped in a way of evaluating things based on the belief that there is an independent source of evil and an independent source of good. Consequently, one generation after another has been conditioned to think and make decisions in an absolutist manner. It has created in people an "either one or the other" mind-set: one is either good or bad, right or wrong. Those possessed of such an attitude - and most seem to be - are living in two mythical worlds that are constantly clashing. Life to them is an ongoing series of dichotomies. In their mind the physical is separate from the spiritual. One's job is not viewed as a suitable place for spiritual expression and development. A church-sponsored class, a monastery, a cave are considered appropriate places.

Along the same line, the body is held in low esteem as compared to the spirit. In fact, in some religions the body is synonymous with sin. Spiritual development, it is believed, comes about by denying or punishing the body. Religious celibacy is based upon that principle. So is flagellation. Because they believe the devil is associated with the body, they feel that by whipping themselves they are flogging the devil. The same attitude is applied to contemplation versus action. You either live in the world of action or the world of contemplation. This kind of mind-set prevailed even among the ancient Greek philosophers and scientists. It is most pronounced in the developing world's universities where social theory, philosophy, law, political science, sociology and psychology - the contemplative courses - are preferred over the action-oriented courses like agriculture or the rural technologies that train students how to build wells, set up irrigation systems and eradicate disease-carrying mosquitoes. Reason versus intuition is another false dichotomy that is accepted in most circles as reality. The reasoning person is viewed as cold and logical, whereas the intuitive person is considered warm, spontaneous and creative. People who are intuitive are felt to be spiritual, whereas the reasoning person is considered less spiritual, more intellectual, scientific.

There are other false dichotomies that are accepted as reality. For example, among the counter-culture groups, laws are considered obstacles to gaining inspiration. Laws, they feel, block the flow of love. Those who value laws are branded impersonal, cold, legalistic, whereas those who reject laws are viewed as spiritual, liberated, free thinkers. In the Baha'i Faith, its adherents are struggling to strip themselves of the either/or syndrome and internalize a view of reality that is to be the basis of a new world order. What they learn expands their mind, opens new vistas of understanding. For some, it is a form of rebirth. Body and spirit are viewed as two aspects of one reality, the body's relationship to the spirit being like the lamp's relationship to the light. It is held that one can attain spiritually by being practical, even wealthy, as long as one isn't attached to his wealth; that action as well as contemplation is necessary in expressing one's faith - building a well in a parched land is a spiritual act as worthy as meditating on the Words of God; that one need not seek a trail of sorrow and suffering in order to grow spiritually, believing that flagellating oneself or climbing a thousand concrete cathedral steps on one's knees is going to guarantee passage into heaven; that one need not be somber to be spiritual; that one could be happy and still be spiritually centered. Happiness is everyone's birthright, attained when we satisfy all our needs - not our fickle wants - and pursue a life of service. Making others happy, and dedicating oneself to the cause of unifying the human race, are profound religious acts.

Those who have abandoned the decline process flow for the growth process flow appreciate and often embrace this type of thinking. No longer skeptical, and no longer plagued by the either/or syndrome, they become active advocates of the steps leading to the Lesser Peace, steps enunciated in God's Minor Plan. Armed with new age knowledge, which they have seen practiced on a community level, they have grown more confident that what Baha'is foresee as mankind's glorious future will materialize. They now understand why they were once skeptical about the prospects of world unity and peace in their lifetime. Based on Cold War era thought and practices, there weren't the means or will to establish peace. Consequently, most people were locked into a pessimistic mind-set. A new set of values was required. As a gift from God - they were made available, and quietly practiced by a few amidst the horrors of past wars and the tumult, the anxiety, and psychological oppression resulting from the Cold War.

15

A Network of Communities

From the start, Baha'is have been involved in a community building process - not a movement. The Baha'i Faith is more than a movement, it is a growing global community composed of men and women aware of their mission to help build a new world order based on a divine blue-print. Inherent in this community are the mechanics of world unity and peace.

Movements come and go, even those that gain extreme popularity. Many movements stem from a collective desire to reform existing conditions, and usually do good things. For example, the Green Peace movement has alerted governments and the average citizen to the dangers of the present-day ecological breakdown in the world. But you can't create a mature community based on one issue, regardless of its importance.

The Civil Rights Movement in America during the 1960s made significant strides in overcoming certain aspects of racism. Laws were passed that ended legalized segregation and overt discrimination. Yet, racism still exists in America. And it will continue to exist until mature communities are established. One of the prerequisites to the development of a mature community is for its citizens to recognize and practice the principle of the oneness of humankind. That principle is the basis of every Baha'i community in the world. Not that all Baha'i communities manifest perfect racial harmony. While they are in varying degrees of development, all of the believers are aware of their responsibility to rid themselves of their prejudices. It is their spiritual duty to do so. Aware of that obligation, the local governing body strives to create the kind of social and spiritual climate that will inspire personal initiative in overcoming one's prejudices. No form of coercion is employed.

Realizing that the believers are in different states of spiritual development, the governing body tries to create an environment which fosters in every Baha'i a desire to overcome their prejudices. The battle is a personal one. While no one monitors a person's progress, the governing body is a constant source of encouragement. It will assist in someone's struggle only if asked to do so. Such requests are not uncommon.

For some Baha'i communities, achieving true unity is a struggle. But, despite the difficulties they face, they know they must continually make every effort to become truly unified. Giving up the struggle is viewed as a rejection of God's will. In dealing with the challenge, it doesn't matter what the social makeup of the community is. There have been cases where racists have embraced the Faith, knowing full well its teaching on racial harmony. Such believers aren't shunned; a sincere effort is made to free them of their racist feelings, employing compassion and patience. On the other hand, the traditional targets of racism find an atmosphere that allows them to overcome a deep seated suspicion of a people who historically have considered them inherently inferior - and at times persecuted them. In the Baha'i community, former Ku Klux Klansmen and Black Panthers eventually embrace - a common spiritual commitment driving them to come together. The only way to avoid the struggle is to leave the Faith. And that rarely happens.

Factionalism in the Baha'i community doesn't exist; any hint of its possible development is immediately addressed. Baha'is view the struggle to attain community harmony as an opportunity to grow spiritually, and participate in the divine drama of establishing a new world order model for living. The struggle to attain community oneness is based on a process that's inherent in the Baha'i teachings. The first step is gaining an understanding of the principle of the oneness of humankind, as well as an appreciation of the principle of unity in diversity. It isn't uniformity that's sought, but rather a unity which appreciates cultural and individual differences. The second step is getting to know one another regardless of one's background or appearance. When that's achieved, the third step follows naturally - people learn to love one another. Those involved in the process know that pain is a by-product of love. Knowing what it will lead to helps them endure it.

True, some movements evolve into communities. Generally, they're exclusive social entities kept together by either the force of a charismatic figure or a philosophy that satisfies some people's special emotional needs. In order to succeed, these communities cut themselves off from the mainstream of life. In time, the leader loses his appeal or dies; or the philosophy no longer fulfills a need, resulting in internal dissension and disorder. Since the advent of Baha'u'llah, thousands of communes were formed, enjoying a short period of success and finally failing, leaving their membership disillusioned, cynical and often in worse shape than when they joined a commune.

Actually, Soviet communism was a grand commune, growing out of a movement that promised the creation of a social and economic heaven on earth. With a proven formula for quick industrialization, communism attracted many adherents in developing countries. In fact, some of those countries adopted the movement's philosophy.

It took 70 years for the community that emerged from the Bolshevik movement to collapse. Conversely, the divinely ordained community that is growing out of the Revelation of Baha'u'llah slowly and steadily - and inconspicuously - gained strength and vitality. The reason for the difference is that brute force was used to keep the Marxist society together, as well as denial of the human being's spiritual nature - it was the latter that broke the dam's wall. In contrast, those building the Baha'i community have chosen freely to follow the path they're on. They are people of all walks of life, motivated by the love of God and guided by His vision of a truly united humanity, where cultural and individual differences are genuinely celebrated.

For decades, the Baha'is activities evoked little public notice because the changes they were making had to do with personal attitude, behavior, a shift of vision - nothing sensational; and the Baha'i community-building effort aroused little interest among the so-called expert social theorists, because they felt what the Baha'is were attempting was a pipe dream enterprise. Nevertheless, the Baha'is kept building. What they were constructing would be the social, economic, political and spiritual bedrock of the new world order. It is the kind of change that comes about when a forest evolves from a single seed. Now, after nearly 150 years of growth, the Baha'i network of communities is beginning to catch the attention of some great thinkers who are aware of the processes of decline and growth operating in the world and who sense the pull towards global unity.

Noted scientist and author George Land is one of them: "The evolutionary reality of nature is moving everything to higher and more complex levels of interconnection and independence. As nature's most successful and evolutionary partner, humanity has now created a complex network of connections that has brought the earth into an independent global village. The principle of entropy maintains that all systems are ultimately headed downhill. The evolutionary evidence of creative growth and change going on within every natural system indicates quite the opposite. The challenge of humanity is to understand that the creative process of nature is pulling all systems including organizations and civilizations to a future different from the past. To align with nature's processes requires being open to making new and different connections with people, ideas, resources and opportunities. The Baha'i Faith is one of nature's 'strange attractors' which holds out the possibility that humanity can bring into being what never existed before. The Bahai's belief in visualizing a creative, powerful peace is in complete alignment with nature's creative process."

In a public address in San Francisco, Ervin Laszlo acknowledged the Baha'i contribution to the development of the new world order: "Baha'is have a particular role and a unique responsibility in bringing about the global society, the fruit of evolutionary convergence among contemporary nations. Baha'is alone among the organized communities of this contemporary world have the practical experience as well as the prophetic guidance for living in a global convergent society. The Baha'is have a responsibility toward the rest of the world ... Not all members of the world community are in a position to offer a practical model to effectively promote this process; but the worldwide Baha'i community is. Hence Baha'is clearly ought to offer themselves and their experience for study by all peoples and nations of this world. The Baha'i community could and should assume the role of a pioneering role model."

16
Some Remarkable Changes

In its statement "The Promise of World Peace," issued in 1985, the Universal House of Justice invited humanity to look at the Baha'i community as a model for establishing world unity. Without unity, it pointed out, there can be no real peace. The Universal House of Justice explained what had to be done in order for our planet to be truly unified: racism needs to be eradicated; religious strife must end; women must gain equal status with men; poverty must be eliminated; equal universal education must be established; a world government must come into being; and an international auxiliary language must be created to improve communications between peoples.

The statement on peace also underscores the need for women and men everywhere to gain a true understanding of the nature of the human being. The present distorted view, it stated, was hampering humans from realizing their potential as peacemakers - and preventing them from recognizing the reality that all people are members of one family. With that understanding, a person becomes a force for unity.

Though many of the world's political leaders, jurists and leading men and women in academe, business, science and the arts have been given a copy of the peace statement - and while it has been widely acclaimed as a profound perspective on how to establish world peace - no government or international peace agency has adopted it as a charter for bringing about real peace; nor has any great world figure led a campaign for nations to endorse it. Nevertheless, Baha'is feel that the statement has been a powerful catalyst for change. Functioning as an instrument of the "Invisible Hand", the peace statement set in motion a wave of change in the world that has left the most noted geopolitical pundits and futurists perplexed. Things that weren't supposed to happen happened.

Consider, again, the state of the world just prior to the revealing of the peace statement: the Cold War's grip on humanity was tightening, inflating the fever of fear everywhere; both sides were swept up in a frenetic arms race that was driving scientists to develop the kind of nuclear attack that would prevent the enemy from retaliating. Work was underway to develop a strike capability from outer space - the ultimate weapon. Because of the security hysteria, the United States doubled its military budget between 1980 and 1985.

In America, the Soviet Union was being hailed as the Evil Empire. In the Soviet Union, America was viewed as the arch-imperialist defender of the rich and oppressor of the poor. NATO and Warsaw Pact armies and navies were swelling in size and arming themselves with more sophisticated weaponry. While more and more intercontinental ballistic missiles were being produced and placed in strategic launching sites, conventional or civil wars were raging in Northwest Africa, in Ethiopia, Mozambique, Cambodia, Afghanistan, El Salvador , Nicaragua, Colombia, Sri Lanka, Southwest Africa, Chad, Angola, Nicaragua, Sudan, and Lebanon was being torn apart by warring internal factions. A new incurable disease called AIDS was becoming a world-wide health menace; the chasm between the poor and rich was widening; homelessness was becoming a critical social problem; and the use and trafficking of drugs was spreading into all strata of society at an alarming rate.

More and more people seemed caught up in a mindless drift, frightened of the future, wallowing in pessimism. Suicide among the youth was on the rise. The old and tested value systems were crumbling, causing more people than ever before to adopt amoral living patterns. It was a time that aptly fit contemporary historian Arnold Toynbee's analysis of what leads to the collapse of a civilization. In his 12-volume "A Study of History," he concludes that all of the past civilizations he studied experienced the same symptoms of decline. Those same signs were apparent in 1985:

The collapse of harmonious relations between the governing minority and the governed majority. Tension and distrust existed between both groups, causing disunity, and eventually hostility, and in some cases - fighting.

The rise of authoritarian and totalitarian regimes, gained by force or terror.

Rise in the number of displaced persons, both the people who flee their homelands because of fear, and the psychologically displaced, who are alienated, who have no sense of belonging.

Large numbers of people caught up in a morbid sense of drift. Their lives move in a negative direction - infected by pessimism, fearful of the future.

Promiscuity. Not only in behavior but in culture as well.

The Universal House of Justice's statement on peace was revealed at a critical time, a time when humanity groaned for deliverance from an agonizing existence and frightful uncertainty. The remarkable changes came like a sudden downpour during a hot, sticky summer's day. A refreshing breeze followed, fanning the clear air. New voices were heard, uttering encouraging words and proposing daring ideas. What humanity witnessed seemed unbelievable.

Three years after the peace statement's issuance, Soviet President Mikhail Gorbachev addressed the United Nations General Assembly. What he said stunned the world, for it was a radical departure from the standard Soviet line. Flowing from him was a vision familiar to Baha'is: "... In a word, the new realities are changing the entire world situation. The differences and contradictions inherited from the past are diminishing or being displaced. But new ones are emerging. Some of the past differences and disputes are losing their importance. But conflicts of a different kind are taking place. Life is making us discard illusions. The very concept of the nature and criteria of progress is changing. It would be naive to think that the problems plaguing mankind today can be solved with the means and methods which were applied or seemed to work in the past. Indeed, mankind has accumulated a wealth of experience in the process of political, economic and social development under highly diverse conditions. But that experience belongs to the practices and to the world that have become or are becoming part of the past. Today, further world progress is only possible through a search for universal human consensus as we move forward to a new world order."

Many of those who heard Gorbachev's speech at the United Nations in December of 1988 were amazed at what he said, because they were aware of his political background. Brought up in a Communist society, and nurtured in Leninist-Marxist philosophy, Gorbachev became an articulate advocate of the Soviet system, so articulate he became his country's supreme ruler.

It's doubtful that when Gorbachev ascended to the leadership of the Soviet Union he was aware of becoming the instrument that would soon deliver the death-blow to his political party. Faithful to his ideological beliefs, he tried hard to prevent what was inevitable. But the forces of change were overwhelming. A practical man, he adjusted to the flow of unprecedented events. Compromise followed compromise, until the Soviet grip on Eastern Europe loosened. Six countries were reborn - free at last, all struggling with functioning within a democracy. Only a year after the Berlin Wall fell, the world looked on in disbelief as Gorbachev stood by helplessly watching his once mighty Soviet Union die, and all of the republics that once constituted the USSR become independent nations desiring affiliation with the European community. The Russian Republic even applied for membership in NATO.

The other superpower leader, U.S. President Ronald Reagan, also found himself doing what was uncharacteristic of him as a politician and statesman. What he did baffled his fellow political ideologues. A staunch nationalist with a deep distrust of communism, a fervid proponent of free enterprise economics, a believer in his country's Manifest Destiny role in the world, and a possessor of a might-makes-right mentality, Reagan suddenly urged his countrymen to accept a series of disarmament treaties with the Soviet Union - that led to the end of the Cold War. What caused Reagan's shift in attitude toward a nation he had denounced as an "evil empire?" It's doubtful that anyone, including Reagan himself, really knows. Of course, hindsight is always sharper than foresight.

Now, all sorts of reasons are being given for the dramatic changes in

Europe. Some conservative analysts feel that Reagan purposely fired-up the arms race in order to break the Soviet economy, thinking that would spark communism's downfall. If that was Reagan's strategy it was a self-destructive strategy, for the arms race turned the United States into the largest debtor nation in the world, and made it more dependent on other nations than ever before. Interestingly, as the Soviet Union and the United States drew closer together, their status as superpowers diminished, and they could do nothing about it. In trying to settle geopolitical disputes, they were forced to look more and more to the United Nations for help. Not only that. They found themselves uncharacteristically appealing for aid: the Soviet Union asking for food and medical supplies from their former enemies as its internal political restructuring effort sputtered along; and the United States asking its European and Middle Eastern allies for financial donations to support its military build-up during the Iraqi crisis.

Though many Americans claim they won the Cold War - no one won it. The "Invisible Hand" broke up the conflict and guided humanity in a different direction - toward its destiny.

The Universal House of Justice peace statement functions as a divine compass, pointing the way to the Lesser Peace. After 1985, the guidance given by the Universal House of Justice took on a life of its own. Mysteriously, the points made in the peace statement received serious worldwide attention by forces that had no connection with the Universal House of Justice. In fact, some of them never heard of the institution. Nations resorted to actions that were uncharacteristic of them. Albania broke out of its self imposed isolation, wanting to interact with the rest of the world; the Union of South Africa freed Nelson Mandela and hundreds of other political prisoners, and decided to abandon its Apartheid system; Vietnam decided to pull its troops out of Cambodia; Cuba did the same in Angola; the Soviets withdrew from Afghanistan; the Libyans left Chad; Iran and Iraq stopped fighting, and the Nicaraguan civil war ended. There was peace in Southwest Africa.

Suddenly, political freedom came to areas of the world that have been suppressed for 45 years. Hungary, Poland, Romania, Czechoslovakia, Bulgaria and Outer Mongolia emerged from the shadow of the Kremlin as truly independent nations. East Germany was willingly annexed to West Germany. The Warsaw Pact was dissolved and NATO became less of a force. Emerging as a new force was the Conference on Security and Cooperation in Europe. On Nov. 21, 1990, 32 European countries and the United States and Canada meet in Paris and signed a charter that proclaimed: "The era of confrontation and division of Europe has ended. We declare that henceforth our relations will be founded on respect and cooperation." They agreed to form a secretariat in Prague, an office in Warsaw to monitor elections, a conflict prevention center in Vienna, and a call was made for the establishment of a CSCE parliament. Drastic cuts in conventional armed forces and weapons were made.

As news of this historic event spread, some people began to sense a federation of states emerging, stretching from Vancouver to Vladivostok, and in time, being joined by the rest of the world's nations. Though only 34 countries participated in the CSCE conference, it was a step in the direction the peace statement points to - that is, the holding of a U.N. sponsored worldwide conclave on peace, with every nation represented.

It is interesting to note that after the peace statement's endorsement of the United Nations as our planet's leading vehicle for the establishment of world peace, a dramatic change took place in the way the United Nations was perceived. Prior to 1985 it seemed politically impotent, unable to stop the wars raging on three continents. Most people, especially in Europe and North America, viewed the United Nations as a battleground for Cold War warriors, who used the institution to manufacture propaganda and persuade non-aligned nations to join their camp.

After 1985 the United Nations began to exercise powers it was created to exercise, gaining results it was expected to gain. Through its efforts the bloody Iraq-Iran dispute was settled; so were the conflagrations in Angola and Namibia; and the United Nations has been making headway in settling disputes in Cambodia, the Sahara, and Afghanistan. With renewed respect, the United Nations was called on to oversee the elections in Nicaragua and Namibia - which were carried out effectively. In 1988, the Nobel Peace Prize was awarded to the U.N. peacekeeping forces stationed around the world. Only the United Nations Secretariat was able to win the release of all the British, French and American hostages being held by Shi'ite Lebanese groups ideologically and financially linked with Iran. In 1992, the United Nations helped to end civil wars in El Salvador and Somalia.

When Iraq seized Kuwait, most of the world, including its former

Cold War adversaries, turned to the United Nations for help; and through it was able to defuse a potentially explosive situation. It localized a war that had the potential of spreading into World War Three, and set a precedent on how to confront future dictators who try to seize another land. But more than that, by settling the Iraqi crisis, the United Nations was recognized by most nations - for the first time - as the supreme peace-developing and peace-keeping force in the world.

17

After the Year 2000

Regardless of what happens in the world, God's Major and Minor Plans are being implemented. The processes of decline and growth are operating, driving humanity forward - often against its will, in a mysterious manner - toward a preordained time - when the world's nations unite into a global commonwealth, bent on serving its citizenry so they are capable of functioning in a planetary society where the oneness of humankind is an accepted fact and every individual and community is striving to establish and maintain the unity of the human family.

Some skeptics may scoff at such a vision, relegating it to the stuffed storage bin of idealistic concepts. That's okay. Because of the rightness of the cause, the opposition will only force the advocates of the vision to strengthen the weaknesses the skeptics cite, thus perfecting whatever God's Minor Plan calls for. Besides, the professional doomsayers have lost their credibility with many people after the Cold War's unexpected end. Their well-reasoned positions were dashed, for they hadn't taken into account the operating force of the "Invisible Hand." Consequently, more people than ever before are rejecting old world order proposed solutions, and are looking elsewhere for direction. While a hopeful sign - for they sense that something greater than themselves is forging humanity's course - they remain insecure because they have no idea of what's in store. While waiting is a test of faith, without any indication of where humanity is headed, people eventually grow restless, and in time, desperate. They seek guidance, something to look forward to, something that will make them more secure, and something they can help implement.

While the guidance inherent in God's Minor Plan is omnipresent, the continuous upheavals and tumult in an ever changing world have distracted humanity from noticing it.

It was alluded to by the Bab, revealed by Baha'u'llah, reiterated by Abdul Baha and propounded by Shoghi Effendi from Mount Carmel, that sacred spot where pilgrims have come awaiting divine direction from a great world redeemer. Baha'is are aware of the guidance and want to share with the rest of the human family what they know, especially what's in store in the future. Aware of the vision penned by Shoghi Effendi in the turbulent 1930s, they are doing their utmost to set the stage for the coming of the Lesser Peace. While working to unite the human family wherever they reside, Baha'is are also involved in the building of the Ark - that same Ark that the ancient prophet Isaiah had envisioned gracing the heart of Mount Carmel: "And it shall come to pass, in the last days, that the mountain of the Lord's house shall be established on the top of the mountains, and shall be exalted above the hills; and that all nations shall flow unto it" The Ark will be God's earthly linkage with mankind, a channel of divine grace with humanity, a center of salvation, if you will. Operating in a series of buildings, positioned in the form of an arc, will be agencies studying, preserving and disseminating various aspects of God's latest revelation to humankind; and coordinating the institutions that have resulted from the revelation. When the Most Great Peace is established, the Ark will become the spiritual and political center of a planetary government, which in time, will evolve into the long-promised Kingdom of God on Earth. The Ark's completion is to coincide with the emergence of the Lesser Peace.

Despite the tensions in the Middle East, construction on Mount Carmel continues. Just as they had faith that the Eastern and Western hemispheres would come together, that communism and Western capitalism would disintegrate as global forces, that humanity would reach maturity and enter the final stage of its social evolution, preparing the way for the Lesser Peace - they are certain that the Ark will be completed.

What will the world be like after the year 2000? Shoghi Effendi provides a penetrating insight: "The unity of the human race, as envisaged by Baha'u'llah, implies the establishment of a world commonwealth in which all nations, races, creeds and classes are closely and permanently united, and in which the autonomy of its state members and the personal freedoms and initiative of the individuals that compose them are definitely and completely safeguarded. This commonwealth must, as far as we can visualize it, consist of a world legislature, whose members will, as the trustees of the whole of mankind, ultimately control the entire resources of all the component nations, and will enact such laws as shall be required to regulate the life, satisfy the needs and adjust the relationships of all races and peoples. A world executive, backed by an international force, will carry out the decisions arrived at, and apply the laws enacted by, this world legislature, and will safeguard the organic unity of the whole commonwealth. A world tribunal will adjudicate and deliver its compulsory and final verdict in all and any disputes that may arise between the various elements constituting this universal system. A mechanism of world intercommunication will be devised, embracing the whole planet, freed from national hindrances and restrictions, and functioning with marvelous swiftness and perfect regularity. A world metropolis will act as the nerve center of a world civilization, the focus towards which the unifying forces of life will converge and from which its energizing influences will radiate. A world language will either be invented or chosen from among the existing languages and will be taught in the schools of all the federated nations as an auxiliary to their mother tongue. A world script, a world literature, a uniform and universal system of currency, of weights and measures, will simplify and facilitate intercourse and understanding among the nations and races of mankind. In such a world, society, science and religion, the two most potent forces in human life, will be reconciled, will cooperate, and will develop harmoniously. The press will, under such a system, while giving full scope to the expression of the diversified views and convictions of mankind, cease to be mischievously manipulated by vested interests, whether private or public, and will be liberated from the influence of contending governments and peoples. The economic resources of the world will be organized, its sources of raw materials will be tapped and fully utilized, its markets will be coordinated and developed, and the distribution of its products will be equitably regulated.

"National rivalries, hatreds, and intrigues will cease, and racial animosity and prejudice will be replaced by racial amity, understanding and cooperation. The causes of religious strife will be permanently removed, economic barriers and restrictions will be completely abolished, and the inordinate distinction between classes will be obliterated. Destitution on the one hand, and gross accumulation of ownership on the other, will disappear. The enormous energy dissipated and wasted on war, whether economic or political, will be consecrated to such ends as will extend the range of human inventions and technical development, to the increase of the productivity of mankind, to the extermination of disease, to the extension of scientific research, to the raising of the standard of physical health, to the sharpening and refinement of the human brain, to the exploitation of the unused and unsuspected resources of the planet, to the prolongation of human life, and to the furtherance of any other agency that can stimulate the intellectual, the moral, and spiritual life of the entire human race.

"A world federal system, ruling the whole earth and exercising unchallengeable authority over its unimaginably vast resources, blending and embodying the ideals of both the East and the West, liberated from the curse of war and its miseries, and bent on the exploitation of all the available sources of energy on the surface of the planet - a system in which Force is made the servant of Justice, whose life is sustained by its universal recognition of one God and by its allegiance to one common revelation - such is the goal towards which humanity, impelled by the unifying forces of life, is moving."

BIBLIOGRAPHY

Brown, Vinson and Willoya, William. *Warriors of the Rainbow.*
Naturgraph + Co. 1962.

Capra, Fritjof. *The Turning Point.* Bantam Books, 1987.

Danesh, H.B. *Unity the Creative Foundation of Peace.* Baha'i Studies
Publications, Ottawa/Fitzhenry-Whiteside, 1986.

Effendi, Shoghi. *God Passes By.* Baha'i Publishing Trust, 1957.

Effendi, Shoghi. *World Order of Baha'u'llah.* Baha'i Publishing
Trust, 1938.

Ferencz, Benjamin B. *Planethood.* Vision Books, 1988.

Gleick, James. *Chaos: Making a New Science.* Penguin Books, 1987.

King, Alexander and Schneider, Bertrand. *The First Global
Revolution: A Report by the Council of the Club of Rome.*
Pantheon Books, 1991.

Land, George. *The Evolution of Reality.* The Journal of Baha'i
Studies, Vol. 3, No. 1, 1990-91.

Murchie, Guy. *The Seven Mysteries of Life: An Exploration in Science
and Philosophy.* Houghton Mifflin, 1979.

Naisbett, John + Aburdene, Patricia. *Megatrends 2000.* William
Morrow and Company, 1990.

Nash, Geoffrey. *The Phoenix and the Ashes.* George Ronald
Publishing, 1986.

O'Driscoll, Herbert. *The Year of the Lord.* Moorehouse Publishing,
1987.

Peck, Scott M. *The Different Drum: Community Making and Peace.* Simon and Schuster, 1987.

Russell, Peter. *The Global Brain.* J.T. Tarcher, 1983.

Rutstein, Nathan. *To a Seeker.* George Ronald Publishing, 1986.

Sahtouris, Elisabet. *Gaia: The Human Journey From Chaos to Cosmos.* Pocket Books, 1989.

Schumacher, E.F. *A Guide for the Perplexed.* Harper & Row, 1977.

Sears, William. *Thief in the Night: The Case of the Missing Millenium.* George Ronald Publishing, 1961.

Tyson, J. *World Peace and World Government From Vision to Reality.* George Ronald Publishing, 1986.

__ *Messengers from the Universal House of Justice 1968-1973.* Baha'i Publishing Trust, 1976.

Reflections